"It's All in Me!"

My Journey to Freedom and Living Abundantly

by

Minister Jalisa Ray

It's All In Me! - My Journey to Freedom & Living Abundantly

Copyright © 2018 Minister Jalisa Ray

Published by: Jalisa Ray International

Printed in the United States of America

All Rights Reserved. No part of this publication may be reproduced, stored in a retrieval system, distributed or transmitted in any form, or by any means – for example, graphics, electronic, mechanical including photocopy, recording, taping – without the prior written consent of the publisher. The only exception is brief quotations in printed reviews, quotes or references.

Editor: Ink Pen Diva Manuscript Critique Services, LLC

Book Cover & Interior Design: William Flowers of Mojo Graphic

Ray, Jalisa

It's All In Me! - My Journey to Freedom & Living Abundantly

ISBN-13 (paperback): 978-0-692-07017-8
ISBN-13 (ebook): 978-0-692-08113-6

Special discounts are available on bulk quantity purchases by book clubs,
associations and special interest groups.

For details email: ministerjalisa@jalisaray.com

or call (240) 343-4177

Acknowledgments

There are many people that have contributed to this book because they contributed to my life. There are people that have been there for me through the good and bad seasons of my life. Some only for the bad seasons, while others for the good. Through it all, I have had the privilege and honor to say that I am **not at all** self-made. It has taken a village to raise and mature me. I would be here all day if I were to acknowledge everyone by name, but I will name a few.

First and foremost, I would not be here today, and I would not be writing this book if it weren't for my Creator, Lord and Savior, and Guide, God the Father, God the Son, and God the Holy Spirit. One in three persons. He has truly been everything to me. Even when I wanted nothing to do with Him, He was still there protecting and providing for me.

My parents Reverend Jervis and Minister Patricia Ray. Without them being willing vessels to carry, nurture, provide, teach, and help me along the way, I do not know where I would be. I could not ask for a better set of parents. They are not perfect, but God knew that they would be the perfect parents for me.

My sister Tianna Tolen who was my second mother growing up and at some points in life my best friend. Through it all, you have been strong, supportive, and loving in the best way you know how. We have had our ups and downs, but I wouldn't have it any other way.

My brother Dante Ray has always been one of the reasons why I push to be the best version of me. He has looked up to me and in some ways, I have looked up to him. He is the best little brother anyone could ask for!

My brother Demetrius Majors aka Meechie has only been in my life for a few years now but has made a true impact on it! I admire his carefree attitude, not allowing the down times in life to get him down!

"It's All in Me!"

He has been through so much, but always manages to keep a smile on his face. He has always been so supportive of me.

There is one other name I MUST mention, or I would be remiss, Mrs. Robyn-Ann Lawson who has been my mentor, coach, and friend being so patient with me throughout this process. She checked in with me every day at 1pm to make sure that I was writing, she encouraged me and sort of forced me to set a date to complete this book. If you look up the definition of accountability you will see her picture! I cannot thank you enough from the bottom of my heart! I am so glad God led me to write you that day, it has truly changed my life! I LOVE YOU SO MUCH! Keep reading you may get mentioned in here somewhere!

To all of my other family, church family, friends, sorority sisters, exs, enemies, and everyone else, THANK YOU from the bottom of my heart! Please do not feel slighted because I did not mention your name, we both know how you have impacted my life and have helped me to become the woman of God that I am today!

About the Author

Minister Jalisa Ray is the epitome of an overcomer. She is the CEO/Founder of *Jalisa Ray International,* formerly, *Empowerment Unabridged*, where she empowers Christ-seeking millennial women of color to obtain financial freedom by providing holistic wealth and money mindset coaching. Born into less than ideal conditions in the ghetto of Buffalo, NY, she didn't allow her upbringing to cause her to become a statistic. When she learned to write at an early age she used it as an outlet for life's many challenges. Being sexually abused as a young child, she wanted to find an outlet. For her, a positive outlet became writing. Min. Ray has written and performed poetry, plays, skits, stories, speeches, sermons, and still uses journaling as self-care to this day.

At 10 years old her parents moved the family to Laurel, Maryland where her journey to find freedom began. With more trials and tribulations happening as she got older, it wasn't until age 20 when she was finally able to begin to tell someone all she had been through. Her first book, *"It's All In Me!" - My Journey to Freedom and Living Abundantly*, was a long time coming. Through some setbacks and hang-ups, it was finally published and released February of 2018. She is excited to share her story with the world of how she overcame by the grace of God, all her tragedies, trials, and tribulations. In her first book, she literally bares it all from start to finish, every embarrassing detail. All about her life, in hopes that her journey to freedom will help the masses on their journey to freedom as well.

Minister Ray has accomplished many things in her life with education, organizations, and more, but her biggest accomplishment so far is this book. She knows that many people will make great strides on their journey to freedom from reading this book. She takes no credit for anything, any compliment she gets for her accomplishments will be returned with an, "All glory to God." She knows that without Him nothing that she's accomplished would be possible.

Table of Contents

Acknowledgments ii
About the Author iv
Table of Contents v
Foreword vi
Introduction 1
Chapter 1: Faith 9
Chapter 2: Family/Friends 29
Chapter 3: Forgiveness/Forgetfulness 55
Chapter 4: Feeding My Mind 73
Chapter 5: Find My Own Path 103
Chapter 6: Reflections 125
Chapter 7: The Abridged Version of my Journey to Freedom and Living Abundantly 129

Foreword

I could tell there was something different about her.

From the day Jalisa popped into my inbox back in 2016 because she purchased a bunch of my courses on purpose and confidence – my heart whispered to "connect with her, she's hungry."

After a chain of emails where she shared her struggles, dreams for ministry, and entrepreneurial vision, I ignored my own business counsel and gave her my direct cell number to chat. I remember telling her not to invest another dime buying more resources until we talked and created a clear plan for her to start ACTING on her dreams. I don't know whether it was her transparency, ambition, or her unique passion for seeing women connect the dots in their health and wealth issues and overcome – but I could tell the enemy was trying really hard to stifle the anointing on this woman. And seeing the devil work this hard to frustrate one of God's daughters made me really mad.

I kept checking up on her until we got to a point where only Ms. Ray could make the decision to drop some baggage to make room for her purpose. Then I backed off and prayed. I knew the new life she craved would cost Jalisa her old life, and that was a big jump that only faith could produce.

Yet, when she reached out to me months later in the Fall of 2017, I could tell she had made that jump mentally. From my experience mentoring dozens of women, I also knew that it was only a matter of time for that spiritual shift to manifest relationally, physically and financially.

It's hard to describe what it looks like when a woman is tired of being tired. Then again, that may be why you have this book in your hand – so you can relate.

There was a new conviction in Jalisa's voice that resonated with my spirit man. A quiet strength. It made me want to surrender even more

"IT'S ALL IN ME!"

to God, in exchange for the peace and confidence that just oozed out of her words. I could tell that she had tapped into an inner power... like she had met the Author of Life Himself and was at peace with the story He was writing about her. Like she knew how the story ended and didn't care anymore about her past or current circumstances – because it was all working for her good anyway. Like she knew that no-one, no, *nothing* could ever separate her from the love of Christ.

It was more than just the 21-day fast or the drastic engagement break-up that made me listen. There was an *authority* resting on her from the Holy Spirit that I don't even think Jalisa herself realized. Authority.

Let me pause here for a second, because we often underestimate this word that Jesus paid such a high price for us to have. Authority – also defined as "lawful permission, power or control" – is yours whether you decide to use it or not beloved. To not use it, means to leave it in the devil's hands for him to steal, kill, and destroy what is rightfully yours. But to use it... Oh my! To use it means once you realize that you have the freedom and right to use it back on him, you realize that everything can and must change.

Listen. Don't let the devil bully you into giving up this privilege, call that liar on his bluff. Blood was shed for this. The bill is paid. The bag is secure. (And yes, I'm talking about much more than money here). Everything you need has already been authorized by heaven. You do have the authority to choose joy each day, and multiple the resources you have to create your destiny. You do have the permission to ask. You do have the power to change. And you can control your actions, walk away, and start fresh again. **It's all in you.**

Which is why the title of this book "It's All in Me" is so fitting. Not only does Jalisa walk you through her story – but she walks you through the practical steps we all must take to pick up our God-Given authority and make it work for us, instead of hell's agenda. Whether it's you, me, your pastor, or Jesus Himself – we all must learn to wield our own

Minister Jalisa Ray

sword of authority. And Jalisa shares this Good News again in such a refreshing and relatable way. She humbly and boldly reminds us that nobody is too broken, or too battered to walk free.

Jalisa was the last woman to enter my mastermind that year - but she was the one that finished her goal in half the time planned. Yes, she stumbled, sighed, and even got scared at times. But she persisted. Though the distractions and hardships didn't stop, she pulled down on grace and wrote a piece of her story each day. She was committed to getting this message out to you, so don't let it go to waste.

Don't just skim this book. Allow the questions and prompts to till the weeds of worry and weariness in your heart, and plant fresh seeds of hope. For this book is more than just a testimonial. This is heaven's victory dance on the devil's head reminding him that he lost another kingdom kid - which was never his to begin with anyway. This is Jesus' war cry to the rest of us to keep pushing and not fall for the enemy's bluffs - past, present, or future - because He's not the one holding any of the keys to your destiny. Not. Even. One.

Jalisa is determined to make God's truth about her a reality, and that's what attracted me to her. She knows that God would not lie to her and is committed to this journey of watching His promises come alive each day. The same is true for you if you have this book in your hand. Something about Jalisa's story or presence makes you want to step into more. Well, that's exactly what Jesus died for you to have…more. "Life and life abundantly" is what the Bible calls it in John 10:10.

So, if you are reading this, it is not too late.

You can still take God seriously about your purpose and agree with who you already are. There is no need to find yourself or fix yourself first, because God knows exactly how to reveal the true you. However, you must decide to **stop making wishes, and start making choices** that give God room to get closer to you. The battle is not yours, but the Lord can only fight for those who choose to stay under His wings.

"It's All in Me!"

While reading Jalisa's book, I remembered my own testimony of overcoming porn and purpose-less living to watch God open doors for me to speak about His deliverance and travel the world for my job. Jesus did not save you to tame you. He rescued you to freely and fearlessly pursue the dreams He painted on your imagination.

It's time to stop settling for bored, blah, broke, and bound up.

It's time to stop fighting with words and fight with THE WORD that never fails.

It's time to roar like there's actually a lion living on the inside of you. Seriously, there is. (Proverbs 28:1)

I don't care how much you feel like it or not friend – these feelings aren't loyal, but God sure is. It's time to tell your emotions who is King. It's time to honor your King by putting your crown of authority back on. Let this book be that turning point for you, the day you decided to let God be true, and every man a liar.

Because everything you've gone through up to this point has only created the perfect backdrop to show off God's might and miracles. So that "your faith should not stand in the wisdom of men, but in the power of God" (1 Corinthians 2:5).

Let's roar.

Robyn-Ann Young

Speaker, Coach, and Founder of UNCAGED Enterprises

Author of the *Women Who Finish* book series

Behold, I have given you authority to tread on serpents and scorpions, and over all the power of the enemy, and nothing shall harm you.

-Luke 10:19

Minister Jalisa Ray

When I first met Jalisa Ray back in 2014, I knew she was special. I found her to be friendly, bright and authentic. As I got to know her better over the past few years, I also learned that she had internalized the principles of good money management and was dedicated to helping others succeed. I've seen her living the concepts that she has written about in "It's All In Me". What impresses me most about her is her humble spirit and giving heart. She's always open to sharing the knowledge she has with others as she continues to learn, grow and develop her skills in her areas of expertise.

In this fantastic freshman book, Jalisa shares poignant and relevant stories to help you gain clarity on your journey to freedom and abundant living. Each chapter and concept are laid out in an order that will lead you to uncover your own strengths and when followed and put into practice will make a positive difference in your life, family and community. She wants you to experience the quality of life that so often seems just out of reach and laying her soul bare will be the catalyst to help you do it.

As a divorced, mother of two sons, I particularly identified with the concepts that the book lays out. My only disappointment is that I didn't have this manual 10 years ago when I faced one of the most traumatic and heart-breaking times in my own life. I firmly believe if I would have had this blueprint, my journey to healing from the pain of betrayal and divorce would have been easier.

I've learned so very much from Jalisa's words. From *"Faith,"* I learned the value in evaluating my relationship with God and allowing him to reveal to me the things that I must surrender to Him to finally be free. Jalisa teaches that God is a gentleman and won't force me to do anything I'm not ready to do, but patiently waits with open arms for me to submit to His will for my life. From the chapter *"Forgiveness/Forgetfulness,"* I am reminded that in order to totally forgive and move forward, we must often choose to forget the hurt that has been dealt. In the chapter *"Feed My Mind,"* Jalisa shares how

"It's All in Me!"

staying grounded in the Word of God daily serves to keep us close to Him.

I am extremely grateful and honored for the opportunity to share a few words about Jalisa and this amazing look into her life experiences. I'm thankful to be her sorority sister and business coach. I know as she so beautifully describes in Chapter 5 *"Find My Own Path"* that all the experiences she's had have worked together for her good and have helped guide her to find her path to freedom. I know that she is grateful for every blessing and every lesson learned along the way.

I encourage you to read this book more than once. Read it to learn about the incredible woman of God who wrote it. Read it to learn how to make a deeper connection with yourself and with God as He guides you to receive His promises over your life. Read it when you're having a particularly tough time dealing with any of the concepts on any given day.

I encourage you to do the journal exercises to help you gain the clarity we all so desperately need on this journey through life. Read it to remind yourself that not only are you not alone on your journey. And finally, read it when you need a reminder that, like Minister Jalisa, you already have all the tools, all the strength, and all the courage you need to succeed inside of you!

Kemberli Stephenson, MBA

Author, Business Coach & Money Mentor

Introduction

February 18, 2017, I turned 26. Where I am from, most of the people my age is either dead, doing drugs, selling drugs, or laying up on welfare making babies. Few of us make it out of Buffalo, NY and really make something of our lives. I can only imagine what my life would have been like, had we stayed in Buffalo and not moved to Maryland when I was almost 11. The thing about the move was that I brought baggage with me I wish I could have left back home.

In my 26 years of life, I have been through many trials and tribulations, but I have also experienced many triumphs and victories. Looking back on my life, I have been able to see how God works all things out for our good. Without the tragedies in life, I would not be as appreciative of the triumphs. I am truly amazed at how God has used me and will continue to use me. This book is only a small portion of the things that God has used me to do. In this book, I will be telling parts of my life story. I will share the strategies I used to overcome adversities and find my path on this journey to freedom and living abundantly. I was taught that every aspect of life is not about a series of destinations, but an ongoing journey. The purpose of this book is to help empower you on your journey to freedom and living abundantly.

In 2013, God gave me the vision for my business *Empowerment Unabridged* now known as *Jalisa Ray International*. At that time, I presented the vision to my pastor Rev. Dr. Tyrone P. Jones, IV and a couple of other mentors of mine. I worked on it here and there, but nothing ever stuck, or I never really stuck with anything. I allowed life to get in the way and I put the vision on the back burner. After trying to do things my way for almost four years, I finally decided to surrender. I would allow God to complete the work He began in me before I was born.

It has not been an easy road. I was not in a place of full surrender until July 30, 2017. Prior to this, I was going back and forth with the idea of being a full-time entrepreneur. I would say, "I am still trying to figure things out," after finishing my 3rd degree and becoming a licensed minister. In order for God to get me to this point, He had to humble and back me into a corner. I was hard headed. I was working at a job making the exact amount that I had written down in my money mindset journal. I left a job that I was happy at with less pay, doing what I loved with children. I had grown to love them as if they were my own. I was content and comfortable. I had planned to be there for at least another two years or so. Then a "better opportunity" came along for advancement and better pay, which was not at all what it was cracked up to be. It was a nightmare from the very beginning. I did not take heed to the signs, well I took heed the money signs, but that was really it.

I knew that I had goals to be debt free by the end of 2017. This extra money was what I thought was going to help me to get there. Wrong! It was the absolute worst job I had ever had! I was only there for two months. People lied on me. People wanted to fight me because of something someone else said. People questioned me about rumors of who was sleeping with who. I switched rooms a few times. I had about five-to-six co-teachers in a matter of those two months. I was being pulled into the office about the drama that occurred, and I began to have migraine headaches every day! Once my health and my state of mind began to deteriorate, I knew that it was time for me to go. After putting in my two-week notice, which turned into almost three out of courtesy for the center, I never looked back.

Once I started having to live off my emergency fund, I glanced back a little. I received multiple confirmations that it was meant for me to be a full-time entrepreneur. Things were not moving as fast as I wanted them to move, nor did they look the way that I wanted them to look. That's where the problem was. It wasn't about when I wanted things to happen or how I wanted them to look. God gave me the vision, so it was to be on His time and the way He wanted things to look. God

"It's All in Me!"

placed many people in my life that have helped me to continue this journey and roller coaster of being a full-time entrepreneur.

My sorority sister, Tasha Hickey, CEO/Founder of Perfect for Purpose, was pushing me in this direction even before quitting my last job. She pushed me to share my business at her launch party for Perfect for Purpose. She even gave me the opportunity to share my services as part of the raffle winnings for the event. She gave me the resources and tools I needed to get my logo done. Even with all of that, I didn't see how things would turn out to be where they are. I planned to still be working my job and building my business on the side. I wasn't taking it seriously, so God knew how to get me to where He wanted me to be as a full-time entrepreneur. He always wants to be able to get the glory out of my story. If I would have stayed at the job and built my business on the side, I would have been trying to take some credit for it. I would have considered myself to be the one "funding my business". So, after settling into the idea in July of 2017 that I would be obedient to God's plan He began to open doors for me.

My passion for *Empowerment Unabridged* was reignited on July 18, 2017, when God led me to post a part of my testimony on Facebook. The post said this,

> *"I have a testimony that includes sexual abuse/incest, multiple instances of rape each time by more than one man, suicidal thoughts, self-diagnosed depression, addiction to sex/pornography/masturbation, promiscuity, alcohol abuse, drugs, rage, hatred, being verbally and physically abusive to my significant others, STD's, multiple near death experiences, being physically and verbally abused, multiple health scares and challenges, and so much more but on*

the other side of it all I am on a journey to holistic health, holistic wealth, and holistic freedom by the grace of God and the blood of Jesus. You may not believe in Him, but I have every reason to. To God be the glory! Someone out there needed this tonight. I wasn't going to post this, but here it is. Your purpose is on the other side of your pain!"

#yourtestimonycanhelpsomeoneelse #gotellitonthemountain #freedomtime #EmpowermentUnabridged"

This act of faith and trusting God led to me being asked to do an interview about my story by Lauren LCThriva. She is doing amazing things in the financial and health and wellness industries. I met her by chance in 2015 at an *Extra Digit Movement* event in Atlanta, hosted by a mutual mentor Brian Beane. EDM is a financial education movement that has changed my life. I became friends with Lauren on Facebook after that event. She inboxed me and said the time I posted my testimony she is normally asleep, but it was meant for her to be up to see my post. Two days later, I was on her show. The topic for that week was "Overcoming Your Giants." I have overcome and am still overcoming giants. One thing I have learned is that my giants are *no match* for God. I don't tell God how big my giants are, I tell my giants how big my God is!

During my time of preparing for the interview, the Holy Spirit brought to my attention "The 5 F's to Overcoming Your Giants," which is what I am going to talk about throughout this book. This was one of the many things that have occurred in my life that led me to this point. I cannot say that there was one particular "turning point" that brought me to actually sit down and write this book. There were many times that God told me to write a book, but I didn't listen. This time I was in

"It's All in Me!"

a place where I was ready to run with the vision God gave me. I was tired of battling with God, because when you battle with God you've already lost. The battle was not Him trying to force me to do something, it was me wanting to hold on to Him and the world at the same time. I wanted Him to be in control of some parts of my life, but not all of them. This book is a declaration of dedication to my journey on the path to freedom, abundance, deliverance, and being fully surrendered to God.

Now, back to the purpose of this book. It will be my testimony of how I overcame. It will also be five strategies that I have used and that you can use in order on your journey to freedom and living abundantly. Here's where the title of the book came from. It was originally something different with the same meaning. The original title was, *My Five F's to Freedom and Living Empowerment Unabridged.* Spring of 2011, I crossed into a Christian sorority, Alpha Nu Omega Sorority, Inc. at Coppin State University. The day that I crossed I was given a new name or my sorority name. The name that was given to me was "Dove Sister Unabridged." The meaning behind why I was given this name was this,

> *"All throughout your life you've experienced many trials and tribulations that others may view as roadblocks. Despite having crushed expectations, personal health struggles, and the necessity to make up schoolwork due to your health absence, you still strive to stay on track with process expectation. Through it all, you managed to push through--you weren't pulled through, you reached inside yourself and through the Holy Spirit you found strength to continue.*

MINISTER JALISA RAY

Because of your great inner strength, you've displayed that you cannot be restricted. Limits cannot be placed on your determination no matter who may try to come up against you. God has shielded you because of the type of assignment He placed on your life. You are both individually capable and complete without having to go to a larger, more complete version for additional consultations. **IT'S ALL IN YOU** *(keep these four words in your heart), the strength, the will, and more importantly, the essence of Christ."*

I am constantly reminded that I am my purpose, so I decided to use my name as part of the name for my business. My business, *Empowerment Unabridged,* is also a part of my purpose. The empowerment portion came from wanting to help you get your power back and help you realize that, "IT'S ALL IN YOU!" That you have the power to change your life to be full and complete, lacking nothing.

After three different people including my editor, who was the first, questioned me about the original title, I decided to divorce myself from it and take suggestions for a different one. One of my business coaches, Kemberli Stephenson and a good friend, Jasmine Linder, helped me come up with the title *"It's All in Me!" - My Journey to Freedom and Living Abundantly.* They told me the original title wouldn't have been understood by most people if they didn't follow me and know what I meant by, "Living *Empowerment Unabridged."* They also told me the original title sounded more like a self-help book instead of a memoir. When my editor, Tamika Sims of InkPen Diva, asked me if I was married to the original title, I was, but after more than one person said the same thing I had to reconsider.

"IT'S ALL IN ME!"

The purpose of this book is to remind you that you have the *exact same* spirit within you that raised Jesus from the dead. Hence the tagline for Empowerment Unabridged, *"Your World is in Your Hands."* We have a choice whether we will live a full and complete life or whether we will live a life of lack and insecurities. Every choice we make moves us forward in our purpose or backwards to our demise. I want this book to empower you to take full responsibility for your life so that you too can be free and live abundantly! I want this book to empower you to overcome your giants. To help you get to a place where you no longer must suffer in silence but have the courage to tell someone about what you have gone through and/or what you are going through. I want this book to help you finally be free from the things that people have done to you. I want you to go from being victims to victors. There is work to be done and you do not have to do it alone! I have overcome and am still overcoming! I want to empower you to know that you can, and you will too! So, as you take a walk with me through these parts of my journey you may cry, laugh, get mad, and more, but you reading this book was Divinely orchestrated by God. It was not by happenstance or by accident. There is something in you that is waiting to be freed, a vision waiting to be birthed, a seed waiting to bear fruit. The time is now for you to be who God called you to be and do what God called you to do! You are not too young or too old. You do not have to wait until your children graduate or until you get enough money. If God has given you the vision, He will give you the provision. Trust me, my life and my business are a testimony of this! So, go be and do it! **NO MORE EXCUSES!** Are you ready? Let's go!

***DISCLAIMER: Some of the things in my story may serve as triggers for you if you have gone through some of the same things that I have gone through. Be prepared to process through those feelings, journal through, and/or have a therapist or someone you can talk through those feelings with on standby.

MINISTER JALISA RAY

Please do not rush through this book! Healing and freedom is a journey, not a destination.***

Chapter 1: Faith

In order to get the most out of your journey to freedom and live abundantly you *MUST* have faith! Your purpose is bigger than you. It is bigger than anything you can even imagine, so you must rely on something bigger than you to accomplish it. In order for your purpose to be planted and grow, you *MUST* have faith. You must believe it, before you see it. When it comes to your faith, seeing it is not believing, believing it, is seeing. You must believe that it is possible before it comes to pass. I am a Christian, so my faith lies in God and His ability to achieve through me, the plan that He has set out before me. He created me and everything else. Why wouldn't I have the faith that He has already completed the work He began in the beginning? When God created the Earth and everything else He did not say, "To be continued…" He said, "It is finished." He looked at everything and said, "It is good." You are finished. You are complete. You are good! Look in the mirror and say, "I am finished. I am complete. I am good!" Yes, it may feel awkward or appear funny, but I am serious! You must reaffirm what God has already done, even if you may not see or feel it. Your past should no longer define you, it never really did to begin with. God created you in His image and in His likeness, *that's* what defines you!

Had it not been for God and my faith in God, although my faith wavered sometimes, I would not be where I am today. He always came through for me! He has never failed me, left me, or given up on me. Like that song says, "Don't give up on God, because He won't give up on you." Faith is like a muscle, the more you use it the stronger it gets. Try it, give your situation, pain, purpose, vision and your life completely to God. Then watch how your faith grows and how you will grow as well. My relationship with God and having a foundation built on Him is what has helped and continues to help me on this journey to freedom and living abundantly. If it weren't for Him I wouldn't have been conceived. My parents were separated when I was conceived up until I was around five years old. It was meant for me to be here and for me to still be here. My whole life has seemed to be a demonstration of the Living Word. What the devil meant for evil, God turned it around for my good. He has and will continue to get the glory from it all. Not only did the enemy try to destroy my parent's marriage, he tried to destroy me in my mother's womb.

My mother had one miscarriage before me. She also had two before my older sister. She had to be sutured with both of us and be on bed rest in order for us to make it through. My sister was a preemie. I was full term, but I was supposed to have major health issues. My mom calls me her miracle baby. Not long into my conception, a routine doctor's appointment turned into a doomsday report for my mom. They told her that I would be born without a stomach and that my esophagus and my windpipe would be fused together. They said I would need multiple major surgeries as soon as I was born in order for me to even have a *chance* at surviving.

Even with the surgeries, there was a huge chance that I would not survive. Not making it through the surgeries was a possibility for me as well. My mother at this time, being a true woman of God, knew that He had the final say. My mom's faith in God kept me here and has led to my faith in God. She decided to go to a revival and had them lay hands on and pray over her as the Bible instructs in James 5:14,

> *"Is anyone among you sick? Let them call the elders of the church to pray over them and anoint them with oil in the name of the Lord."*

"It's All in Me!"

A little while later, she went back to the doctor and all the original health problems they diagnosed me with, were gone. With all the tests and retests, they had done, they could not understand it. My mom knew it was all God. If it weren't for my faith-filled, believing, praying mother and a God who already planned my destiny, I would not have made it. To have gone all those months without a stomach, I was born weighing 6 lbs. and 6 oz. The biggest health scare was out of the way, but there were still some impending health dangers that my mom dealt with after I was born. From that day until I was eight months old, I vomited every time I ate. The doctors could not tell my mother why. They thought it was my stomach and the type of milk I was drinking so they changed my milk over and over. It took many hospital visits and three different doctors for them to figure out that I had asthma. This was an entirely different journey than it was supposed to be initially, but still very scary for my parents. My mom lost jobs because I was constantly in and out of the hospital due to the asthma. She struggled financially taking care of my sister and I, basically on her own, for the first five years of my life, there were years she had to rely on welfare.

I was told that in spite of the asthma I was still a crier, a long crier that didn't cry myself to sleep. I just kept crying unless I was eating or being held. Not understanding or realizing at the time, that it was because of the environment I was conceived in and the condition of the spiritual life of my father at the time. My father was not really in the church, he was out running the streets doing anything and everything he was big and bad enough to do. Hence why my parents were separated for five and a half years. Having a mom who was living for God is what made it possible for me to be who God created me to be. Her faith led to my faith and belief that without God I would not have made it. Without Him, I am nothing. But even living for God, my mother's pregnancy was very stressful dealing with my dad and his mess, which greatly impacted me.

Minister Jalisa Ray

    Growing up I did not really have a relationship with my father because of all the stress, hurt, and drama that he put my mother through. He was not home with me full time growing up like he was with my sister. He missed out on a lot of critical bonding time in my life. He did what he could, but not being at home made an enormous difference in my life. He would visit every day, but when he stayed too long, I would ask my mom, "When is daddy going home?" Also, being sick and my mom not being able to work, I spent most of my time with her building a very strong bond. I do not remember much of my childhood. Because of the trauma that I dealt with I blocked most of it out.

    Here's the thing, my father wasn't born or raised in the church. Even when he began to go to church, the church was not really in him. So, because my dad was not in his proper place and position under God, it affected me as the seed that was planted at my conception. I was conceived and born into corruption. A lot of the things that I dealt with and experienced at an early age, I would not have if my father had been in his proper position in our family. For a long time, I blamed him for it, which I will talk about later in the chapter about forgiveness/forgetfulness. This among other things is why family/marriage and the proper family structure are so important to me.

    As I mentioned in the introduction, I was exposed to a lot of things that nourished the corruption planted at my conception. For years as a young child I was sexually abused by my biological older sister who is almost four years older than I. The sad thing is, she was only doing to me what was being done to her... When my dad came back home he brought a lot of baggage with him. He was addicted to pornography. At the time they came in the form of movies and magazines. He had pornography magazines all over the house, which my sister found and showed to me. The things that she saw in the magazines she would have us do together. This led to exploring masturbation on my own and going to look at the magazines on my own. This led to my addiction to pornography and masturbation as I

"It's All in Me!"

got older. My father also was not faithful to my mother up until I was around the age of 10 years old. I saw him as the example of a man and a minister in my home. This led to me having no respect for men, some ministers, or for myself.

In elementary school I began to explore the world of boys. I can recall my first "boyfriend" in pre-K, his first name was Eric, I don't remember his last name. We would touch each other's private parts and even hump during play time where we played "house." I was considered to be a, "fast little girl," but looking back, my family and I now understand why. On my shoulders and in my soul, laid years' worth of generational curses and soul-ties from past generations. This all led to a life of promiscuity, drug and alcohol abuse, and more, but from my grades and my activity in church no one ever really knew. Of course, my parents did because I lived with them, but my church family and most of my immediate family had no clue. I was able to live a double life. This double life led me to having direct physical/spiritual ungodly soul ties to almost 40 different men and emotional/mental ungodly soul-ties to probably 40 more.

One thing that I learned as I got older is that you not only receive soul ties to that person, but also the people they have slept with and the people they have slept with before you, and so on. So, I had ungodly soul ties to thousands of men and women. Most of which I do not know. Think about it, that girl or guy you don't like for no reason could be because of an indirect ungodly soul tie.

Let's unpack soul ties a little more before we move on. Soul ties can be Godly and ungodly. The Godly ones are orchestrated and destined for you by God. The ungodly ones are those the enemy intends to use to kill, steal, and destroy. They are not only physical, they can be spiritual, mental, emotional, and even financial. The term soul ties is not in the Bible, but it is explained there as becoming one with someone that you should not have, idolatry, and being unequally yoked with an unbeliever. When we are connected to someone or something that God did not intend for us to be connected to whether spiritually, mentally, physically, and/or financially it is an ungodly soul tie. We have Godly soul ties to the people and things that God gives us in order to fulfill the purpose He has given to each of us. Any relationship or material thing that God gives us belongs to Him. Those things can even become ungodly soul ties if we put them before God. If we use them to fulfill our desires instead of for the glory of God. If we find ourselves obsessing over, not being willing or able to let go of, and/or running to them before God, that's how we know something has become an ungodly soul tie. There are other signs and indicators that something or someone has become or is an ungodly soul tie, I just mentioned a few. It is important to always be mindful of the intent for which we allow or keep certain things or people in our lives.

So, with the generational curses, my family's soul ties, and the ungodly soul ties of my own, to some and even to myself I was destined for failure, destruction, and death. The enemy almost succeeded time after time in his mission to kill, steal, and destroy me. Again, God had the final say! Even though I was birthed in corruption, the faith that my mother had and the fact that she prayed over me and gave me back to God has kept me. The faith that she had and the faith that she instilled in me brought me back to Him. This faith is what has freed me from all of those soul ties and has set me on the path to be the one to break the generational curses in my family. I no longer harbor unforgiveness and ill-feelings toward my sister, my parents, or the guys that raped, took advantage of, abused me, and broke my heart. My faith allowed me to forgive, forget, and take responsibility for how I responded to the things that happened to me. My faith is what has allowed me to take back the control I gave to the enemy over my life. I gave it back to God who was really in true control the entire time. Things could have been much worse, and I could have died in my sin, but God said no. I have a story to tell in which I am blessed for you to be reading right now. I know that God has and will continue to work things out for my good. He has

"It's All in Me!"

done the same for you. You have heard part of my story and my journey to freedom and living abundantly through faith. Here's how you can do the same:

1. Evaluate where you are in your relationship with God.

In order to evaluate where you are in your relationship with God, ask Him. He will begin to reveal to you the areas in your life that you have to surrender to Him in order for Him to work on them. One thing that I was always told is that God is a gentleman. He will not force you to hand things over to Him. He will however let it be known through other people, His Word, life circumstances, dreams, visions, and signs that there is something that He has to say to you. If you are not hearing from God, then there are some distractions that you need to eliminate from your life. This can include television, social media, music, certain people, a responsibility that you took on that doesn't fit your purpose, food, makeup, cars, or shoes. Anything could be preventing you from hearing from God. God wants us to be set apart as His children so those things and ways of the world we tend to hold onto may be what's keeping us from building our relationship with Him. *Ask yourself how much am I really willing to sacrifice for my relationship with God? How much have I sacrificed? How much should I be willing to sacrifice?* Another thing that could be preventing you from hearing from Him is that you're not sitting still long enough to hear from Him.

This one right here I have a tough time with myself. I have so many things going on in my life and in my head, that it is a challenge for me to sit quietly to hear from Him. This is something that you must continuously practice and train yourself to do. In order to build your relationship with God, communication is key. Not only should you take time to listen to Him but talk to Him as well. He should be the first one you run to, to talk to. Not only when something is wrong, but about anything. He cares about every single detail of your life. He knows exactly how many hairs are on your head, how many tears you've cried, and every other small detail about you and your life. He created you. In order to get answers about your life, He's the best person to go to. He will show you and tell you where you are in your current location with Him and in your life. He will let you know whether you are on the right path or not and will redirect you as needed. God allows U-turns! Your relationship with God is the foundation of all your other relationships. Once you can get to a place where your relationship with God is healthy and flourishing, then it will be a whole lot easier to build relationships with other people.

In building your relationship with Him, you will learn about yourself, and how to maintain relationships with other people. We are created and designed for relationship. We were not created to do life alone. Even as an introvert we still need relationships in order to live the full and abundant life that God has called us to. There is so much that we miss out on by trying to do life alone. We make life much more difficult by not sharing our lives with other people. Yes, there is a chance that people will hurt, misuse and abuse you, and anything else. But there is a better chance that God will send people to you that will love, care for, teach, nourish, and pour into you, and you will be able to do the same for others.

Go into your relationship with God and other people with the idea to just be with them. Being with someone builds a connection and a bond like no other. In that state, you are completely focused on that person and not distracted by anything else. You are able to learn things about them that you wouldn't have learned otherwise. In just being with someone, you will see what is needed to be done, but it will be genuine and simple. Building and maintaining relationships should not be as hard as we make it out to be. When you go into the relationship with the best interest of the other person first and not about what you can get out of the relationship, then and only then will your relationship with

"It's All in Me!"

God and others be sustainable and healthy. That's true love, doing things for people without expecting anything in return.

2. Look back over your life and see where God has brought you from.

Your past is one of the best teachers. It is only a fraction of your life, but it makes up your beliefs, habits, values, mindset, thought process, view of the world, and view of yourself. If we have a negative perspective on the past, things that we did, things that were done to us, and things that we thought would happen, but didn't, we will live in a negative state of mind and being. We will have a negative perspective of the past. In order to prevent that, the best thing to do is, as I said earlier, to take full responsibility for your past and how you choose to respond to it, learn from it, and move on. Do not stay stuck in your past. When the time comes, address it. It is also a great idea to get a therapist or a counselor to help you get through this process especially when it includes trauma and significant events in your life that still greatly impact you today. I have had to do this at several points in my life because there were things that I thought I had healed from and gotten over, but certain triggers set me off and took me into very dark places.

At the time of this publication, the most recent run in with my past occurred when I was dealing with a lot of stress around trying to "figure out" what to do with my life. I was also going through an extremely hurtful and emotional situation with my future husband. You'll hear more about him in the next chapter. Our relationship had been on a serious emotional rollercoaster. I allowed a situation to take me to a place of rage and anger that I had not been, probably since I was a teenager. I'll talk a little bit more about this incident in the next chapter as well. I realized then that there were some deep-rooted things that I had not dealt with properly. I realized that even though I said that

I had forgiven him, I really hadn't. I also realized that I had a very negative perspective of him and our relationship overall.

What I was focusing on was being magnified and it caused a buildup of hurt, anger, and rage that all came bubbling up and out at once. I have been journaling for as long as I can remember, I have done exercises at events about forgiving and letting things go. I have had counseling sessions, been prayed over and laid hands on many times. I say that to say that dealing with and healing from your past is, I dare say, a lifelong process that is not going to happen overnight. This is also a reminder to be kind, compassionate, and forgiving with other people because you never know what someone else has gone through or how they perceive the world.

3. **Acknowledge it and ask God to help you let it go. Take responsibility for how you will respond to it and use it from now on.**

In looking back over your life to see where God has brought you from, you have really done the next step, you've acknowledged your past. Acknowledging it, it keeps you from going to the place where you believe that, "If I ignore it, it will go away." Those things that hurt you, scared you, wounded you, broke you, and took pieces of you, will not just go away if you ignore it. It will not heal on its own, if you do not give it what it needs to heal. It is like a cancer or an infection if you ignore it, instead of treating it properly it will only grow and spread. Eventually it will kill you, spiritually, mentally, or even physically.

Our whole being is connected, so if something is affecting you spiritually, mentally, and/or physically, it is affecting your entire being one way or another. These strategies are ways to help you get to the root cause of the things that are keeping you from living abundantly.

"It's All in Me!"

The Bible says we have not because we ask not. *Have you asked God to help you to let go of and heal from the things that have kept you in bondage? Have you asked God to reveal these things to you, so you will know exactly what it is that you need to let go of?* This is a part of taking responsibility for the things that have occurred in your life. For me, some of the things that I had to acknowledge and take responsibility for were, how I decided to live my life and treat people after being sexually abused as a child, being raped three times between ages 13-18, and being verbally and physically abused.

I had to acknowledge that I cannot change what happened to me, but I can take responsibility for how I move on from it. I decided that I would move on as a victor and not a victim. I decided that I would not blame my sister for what occurred because I found out that there were other women in our family sexually abusing her. She was doing to me what seemed to be natural or normal to her. We were children. It took until I was 20 years old to tell anyone about the childhood sexual abuse and the rapes that I had survived. That was when my true healing began when I was able to finally open up and tell someone. From there, I have been able to help my family and other people I have met begin their journey to freedom from similar things. They were finally able to tell someone after hearing my story. They no longer have to suffer in silence.

4. **Look for ways that will help you to strengthen your relationship and faith in God. Read His Word, seek spiritual guidance/mentorship, look for a fellowship of believers to join and get involved with. Seek out people that you can help mentor or give back to. When you have a decision to make, seek His guidance and move in faith even in the face of fear.**

Minister Jalisa Ray

Looking for ways that will help you to strengthen your relationship and faith in God involves you not just being with Him, but actually allowing Him to use you and pour into you. I mentioned a few things earlier that I've done and still do, but you must find the things that work for you. There are so many things that can help, but because of the world we live in, the sin-filled world, there is a lot of false information, false prophets, false teachers, and fraudulent organizations that may seem God centered, and God focused but are really not. I have truly been blessed to have the resources and relationships that help to build my faith and strengthen my relationship with God. Your relationship with God is the foundation of, or should be, the foundation of all other relationships. Your relationship with Him will strengthen your relationship with others. Your relationship with Him will help you build and maintain your relationship and connection with yourself. If you feel that you have a hard time hearing His voice, one way to hear directly from Him is to read His Word. The Bible is His Word directly for and to us. Some people feel that it is outdated, boring or not related to them. That is when you need to ask God to make it come alive to you, ask Him to make it clear to you, ask Him to make it plain to you so that you will understand and have a desire to study and learn from it. Do not get caught up in just listening to what someone else may say in a teaching or a sermon. You must study it for yourself. They are human, and they can get it wrong.

The Word of God is active and alive! You should feel as if you are starving without it, like you just cannot live without it. It is indeed our daily bread! Some of the things that I do to make sure that I study and read His Word daily are the *Youversion Bible* app and read devotionals. I watch the videos on the *Youversion* app. I use another Bible meditation app called *Abide* where you get a word and a prayer then they prompt me to journal. I attend Bible Study Fellowship which is a in-person weekly in-depth Bible study, lecture, and discussion that I love. I have also availed myself for opportunities to teach and speak

"It's All in Me!"

about His Word. This forces me to study so that I teach the Truth instead of my opinions and interpretations. There are so many tools and resources out there to help you on your journey to faith and building your relationship with Him. One of the things that I have been doing for some years now is fasting. I did the Daniel fast a few years with my church and I have fasted with my Christian Sorority, Alpha Nu Omega Sorority, Inc. We participate in a fast every 1st and 3rd Wednesday, and I have done absolute fasts. In August of 2017, I did an absolute fast for 21 days and that experience was one of the times where I felt closer to God than I ever have in my entire life. It was a true God experience that I would want everyone to have. It was life-changing! It was during a time when I felt as if my life was heading down a dark path. I believe He called me to it because He knew that I needed to purge and release some things in order to focus on what He has called me to do. One of which is writing this book, and another is building out the vision He gave me for the business.

There is no substitute for fasting. The Bible talks about some things only moving through prayer and fasting. I believe that there were things in my life that would only be moved through prayer and fasting. There were generational curses and soul ties that had a hold on me that would only be moved through prayer and fasting. There were things that I was holding on to that would only be moved and be able to to let go of through prayer and fasting. After the 21-day experience, my faith went to a level that I have never experienced in all of my days. To be in a place of true peace and surrender, that is how you know your faith has matured. It helped me to stop worrying about the provision, the plan that I had put in place for my life, the way I thought things should look, the perceptions that I had of things and just be with Him and allow Him to use and move through me.

5. Truly and totally surrender your life to Him. This does not require you to do anything, but to just be with Him. Allow Him to move and do things in your life and through you.

Allowing God to take over and truly surrendering your life to Him is an act of true faith! It does not require you to try to do anything or try to figure anything out. God does not want or need anything from us. He can do everything without us. He chooses to use us for His work. His love for us grants us the opportunity to be used by Him in ways that we could not even imagine. When you surrender to Him, you will begin to see things as He sees them, doors that you didn't even know existed will begin to open up. Things that you didn't even know to ask for will begin to be poured into your life. People that you didn't even know you needed will begin to show up in your life. Things will begin to move and shift in a way that you have never seen before. The Heavens will open up and you will be in position to receive all the blessings and the inheritance that has your name on it as a child of God. You will realize that just as He takes care of the birds, bees, animals, and trees that He will take care of you even more. He sacrificed His Only Son for you! There is *no good thing* that He will withhold from you. If you do not receive it, then it is not good for you or it is not good for you right now.

There is nothing that you need to worry about, there is nothing that you need to doubt or be afraid of. He has everything under control. All He wants is for you to be with Him. Bask in His glory and in His presence. Worship Him in spirit and in truth. I was in a place before embarking on the 21-day fasting journey where I had surrendered only the things that I wanted Him to take care of. Other things I held on to as if I could do better than Him with that situation, relationship, or circumstance. This fast truly humbled and reminded me that yes, my world is in my hands, but *the* world is in His hands so ultimately, He still has all control. He gives us free will and the ability to choose, but the outcome of things is all in His hands. He wants nothing but the best

"It's All in Me!"

for us and He wishes that none of us perish, but we all have a choice. We can either choose life in Him or death in the enemy.

Contrary to popular belief, when it comes to God there are no shades of gray and no blurred lines. There is no compromise when it comes to living for Him. We can no longer make excuses for being lukewarm. He prefers for us to be hot or cold. There is no more time to, "play church," or pretend to be a Christian on Saturday or Sunday but live a life like the world during the week. Being truly surrendered and walking in faith means to look, think, and act completely different from the world as the peculiar people He made us to be. He made us in His image and likeness. We are not made to live like the world. We are set apart for the things that He has created us to do. My experience with being truly surrendered looks like not having a plan for every aspect of my life and business, but taking things one day at a time, one moment at a time, allowing God to lead and guide me with every move that I make. I cannot breathe without His allowance. I cannot move without His allowance. Anything that I do is only because He allows and makes it so. If He is not in control, then we give the enemy control. I was tired of allowing the enemy to have control over my mind, thoughts, relationships, finances, ministry, business, family, and legacy.

I made a decision to take back everything that I gave to the enemy. That is the only way he could take things from me, is if I gave them to him. I took responsibility for this and truly surrendered to God *every* part of my life. No, I have not "arrived." I am on a journey just like you. I just know that at this point in my life, I am sold out for Him! I just wish I would have figured this out a long time ago. Because I was hard headed, I had to learn the hard way. No matter how many sermons I listened to, how many Bible studies I sat in, no matter how many warning signs I received, I still wanted to do things my way. I ended up falling on my face every time. My mom's famous saying to me was, "A hard head makes a soft butt." That was her way of saying to me that when you're hard headed there is a consequence and you will pay for it one way or another. 26 years later, I *finally* got it. It's not about what things look like or how I want things to look. Walking in faith is just being with Him. Why do we choose to take the harder way? No, this way is not necessarily easy especially with the world that we live in, but it is most definitely worth it.

It may be difficult at first to not try to do anything, but as I said, it is a journey and it takes training and practice. Do not give up. Keep moving forward and things will begin to flow. The Holy Spirit will be in the driver's seat and you will be able to enjoy the ride. You will not have to direct from the passenger seat or even try to see or figure out where you are going. Just enjoy the ride. God is not your co-pilot and you are not His. He does not need your help, just let Him do what He does and that is be God. When it comes to building your relationship with God and building your faith there are many ways to do so, you have to find what works for you. Figure out the best way for you to get to a place of true surrender and being with God. Do not give up. It will be a fight with your old self and the enemy, but you already have the victory! You are a winner, an overcomer, a child of the King! He wants you, all of you, to be with you. He is not hiding, you do not have to chase Him, or really even look for Him. He is right where you are waiting for you with open arms. Make Him your focus and number one priority. It will be the best thing that you will ever do in your entire life. I am a living witness.

"It's All in Me!"

Reflection Questions:

1. How would you rate your faith on a scale of 1-5? (1 being little to no faith; 5 being great faith) Why?

_____
_____
_____
_____

2. If not already, what would it feel like for your faith to be a 5?

_____
_____
_____
_____
_____

3. If not already, what are some of the things you could do to increase your faith to a 5?

_____
_____

Minister Jalisa Ray

My Prayer for You:

Dear God,

The person that is reading this needs You! They need You like never before. They have a thirst and desire for You and only You. They have tried to fill the void for you with many other things, but that never satisfied them. They are running back to you, surrendering it all to you today and everyday moving forward. They are on a journey to freedom and truly living abundantly. True freedom only comes through You. Help them to let go of those things that have been keeping them from truly taking a hold of You. Reach deep down into those dark places and expose those things that they have buried in an attempt to heal and feel whole. I speak deliverance from all soul ties and bondage in their life. I speak peace of mind over every situation or circumstance that may have them worried or afraid. I speak complete healing and wholeness over their life, family, and anything and anyone that is attached to them. I speak the release of strongholds and bondage. I speak growth of the mustard seed faith in them right now in Your name. I speak the ability to receive and give unconditional love in their lives. I speak the release of all generational curses in their life and in their bloodline. I speak generational blessings over them. God, I ask that this this prayer spark a fire in their souls to just constantly be with you. I ask that you just lead them every step of the way and that each step they take be in Your will for their lives. I pray that their relationship with You becomes the most important One to them. I pray that they find just what they need in Your Word, Your people, and Your presence. I pray that they

"It's All in Me!"

glean what they need from their past and are able to move forward in true faith in You. I thank You for their life. I thank You for the blessings and the doors that are about to be opened in their life. I thank You for the overflow of blessings so that they will be a blessing to someone else. I thank You that in you all of their desires are satisfied in the appropriate time. I thank You for giving them a heart of expectation and not anxiousness when it comes to You and the things that You have already done in their life even the things that they have yet to see. I thank You for the purpose and the gifts that You have given them and that from this day forward that they will walk in them with boldness and confidence in You. Thank You for giving us the opportunity to just be with You. Have Your way in their life God! Let Your will be done! You are worthy to be praised!

In Jesus' holy and matchless name,

Amen.

Chapter 2: Family/Friends

> *9 Two are better than one, because they have a good return for their labor:*
>
> *10 If either of them falls down, one can help the other up. But pity anyone who falls and has no one to help them up.*
>
> *11 Also, if two lie down together, they will keep warm. But how can one keep warm alone?*
>
> *12 Though one may be overpowered, two can defend themselves. A cord of three strands is not quickly broken.*
>
> **Ecclesiastes 4:9-12**

This passage of Scripture has always reminded me that life is better when we do not have to do it alone. As discussed earlier, a relationship with God first is fundamental and foundational to having successful and flourishing relationships. One thing we have to remember about relationships are that some are for reasons, seasons, and others are for a lifetime. All of the relationships in our life are not meant to be lifelong. There are relationships we hold on to or we allow to hold on to us longer than we're supposed to. Some that we were not even supposed to enter into to begin with.

In my life, I have had a plethora of relationships with people. I was discussing with my therapist about feeling like I only had seasonal friends or that I am only a seasonal friend because I do not have friends that I have been friends with since I was in elementary or middle school. She asked me if this is a problem and for me it hasn't been. She also asked me if there was a void there and for me that also isn't the case.

Let me first explain what I consider to be a seasonal friend before talking about the people I have in my life in this season. I consider myself to be a seasonal friend or only have seasonal friends because for me it is hard to maintain relationships with people once the season of life is over that we were around it on a regular basis. Once that is over, it is like out of sight, out of mind. I have always been what some consider a "busy body," so once a new season begins and I take on new responsibilities and roles, I begin new relationships and the ones from previous seasons in my life are no longer in the forefront of my mind.

Every now and then someone will come to mind, and I will check on them or they'll check on me. Also, if I am aware of a big event or something that a friend is doing I will do my best to support. I think all my friends know or at least I hope they know that if they need me and I can be there, I will be there. The difficult thing for me, because I have connected with so many people throughout my life, is to try to keep in contact with or keep up with all of those people. In most cases, other than guys I have dealt with, my relationships have not ended on bad terms they just faded as life moved on. There has never been any love lost on my end even if from the other person's perspective, we ended our relationship on bad terms. Once I call someone a friend or build a love for someone then that's that. You're my friend and I love you.

For me, it has never really been difficult to connect with people, even people I just met because I am able to discern or kind of read people's energy. As an introvert it can be uncomfortable, but it is not something I avoid all together. Once I observe and kind of feel people out, I can connect and begin to establish a relationship with someone. From the point of that initial connection to when the relationship fades out, I had not ever really evaluated how or why that happens. I had never been taught how to build or sustain relationships, which I have learned are an essential part of life. Prior to the recent years in my life, I did not consider how important my relationship with God was in building my relationships with other people. Especially with my future husband

"It's All in Me!"

because that relationship should be a reflection of Christ and the Church or in other words Christ and I.

I participated in a webinar whose focus was on building relationships and one person's take on the process of it. It was very strategic. The webinar talked about how important it was to be intentional about building friendships. The webinar talked about the nature of friendships and the questions that should be asked as you progress through the levels of friendship. My entire life I allowed my relationships to grow organically, not really putting much thought into them or planning out relationships with people other than my significant others. To me, that is kind of an awkward conversation to have with someone. To ask someone, "So where do you see our friendship going?" I think I would get a weird look or, an, "I don't know," response.

Maybe that's just me because I would give someone a weird look and an I don't know response (lol). These are the types of questions the webinar suggested we ask. It talked about what love looks like in friendships. For me, this is not an issue. I have a genuine love for people and relationships. At times, this has been a disadvantage for me because people have taken advantage of me, but I did not allow that to change my love for people all together. Although loving others is not a challenge, I have had trust issues. But by building my relationship with God, I was able to overcome those trust issues and still love people the best way I know how. Going back to the Scripture from the beginning of this chapter, it talks about when you work together you get a better return for your labor. By working together, the quality of work is better and what comes out of the work being done together is more than what you would get by working alone. That Scripture and webinar I mentioned before reinforced how important friends are in my life and business.

I have an amazing group of people in my life at this point that are truly a blessing and that allow me to be a blessing to them. There is my mother of course who has actually been my best friend since birth now that I think about it! As I mentioned in the acknowledgements, if you haven't read it shame on you, you might be mentioned in there somewhere, if it were not for my business coach/mentor and 100's of other people in my life that encouraged me to write a book even from an early age, this would not have been possible. My business coach literally checked in with me every weekday to see if I was writing for an hour to complete this book. She held me accountable because I said I wanted to write a book and finish it in 90 days. She encouraged me to set an actual date. She sat on video chat with me and had me set an exact time I would write every weekday and to set a specific date for when I would finish this book. If it weren't for her, I would have still been saying I want to write my first book in 90 days, but probably would have never gotten started for the umpteenth time I had said I was going to write a book, but never did.

    The quality of my book and my business is better because I do not have to do it alone. Having a business coach/mentor that is easily accessible and available has made a world of difference this time around building a business. It also has a lot to do with where I am spiritually and mentally as well because previously I have tried to build businesses where I had mentors and coaches that worked very closely with me, but I did not make much progress or any progress at all. This is what makes me realize that we cannot just deal with things in one aspect of our lives because we are a being that has more than one part. We are spirit, soul, and body. All throughout my life starting with my mother, I have had people in my life that have encouraged, pushed, supported me, and have been there to pick me up when I fall. Like the tenth verse of the fourth chapter of Ecclesiastes says,

> *10 "If either of them falls down, one can help the other up. But pity anyone who falls and has no one to help them up."*

"It's All in Me!"

Had I not had someone there every time I fell to pick me up, I would not have made it to this place in my life. I can recall many times in my life where I was in a depressed state of mind and I did not want to do anything I did not want to leave my room. I lived on campus at Coppin State University in Baltimore, MD and some of my time there I didn't have a roommate. I would actually pray to God and ask Him to just take me away from here. I wanted to die, but I knew that I believed that suicide is a sin, so I would never go as far as to do it or even attempt to do it. I also knew that I believed that I would go to hell if I did commit suicide. My line sisters from Alpha Nu Omega Sorority, Inc. would come to my room, banging on my door until I answered, or they would get an RA to open my door. Those were times where I had fallen. If I had not had someone to pick me up, who knows how long I would have been down. Verse 12 of this passage of Scripture goes on to further explain how important relationships are, not only with people, but with God.

> 12 "Though one may be overpowered, two can defend themselves. A cord of three strands is not quickly broken."

Being alone, those depressed thoughts and feelings would have overpowered me. With God on my side and with people in my life to help me, I was able to defend myself against those thoughts and feelings. I can think of hundreds more situations. Another one is with my future husband who I mentioned earlier. We became friends on a whim through a friend of his, whom I had slept with prior to us becoming friends. I didn't really think anything of it. At the time, I had a boyfriend off campus who lived almost an hour away close to DC. I was living on a college campus, in a long-distance relationship, being a promiscuous teenage girl. I went to college not long after having turned 17 years old. I went off to college early because I had graduated high school a year early. As I mentioned, I had slept with my future husband's friend. My future husband is Anthony J. Hardy also known as "AJ" to most. I will explain why I call him my future husband later as well. Anyway, we became really close friends over a span of three years. During that time, I had a boyfriend, so we were genuinely just friends.

The boyfriend I had at the time I shouldn't have been with to begin with. Our relationship became abusive. I got into a bad car accident that had it been a little bit different, literally by a couple of inches, I could have lost my life or been badly injured. I walked away from the accident with just a slight headache from my head hitting the window. Through all the drama and the tears AJ was there the whole time. My mom kept telling me that he was going to be my husband and that no one would love me the way that he does. I kept telling her no because, at the time, I had a "type."

I wanted my man to be tall, dark, handsome, with long hair, and muscular. AJ was average height, brown skinned, with a teddy bear body type. He looked a lot like Ruben Studdard and that's what some people on campus at Coppin started calling him "Ruben." He was exactly the opposite of what I wanted, but *everything* that I needed in a man. He is caring, loving, has a big heart, and will help anyone and everyone even to the point of being taken advantage of. Even with a boyfriend anything I asked him to do he did. He is funny, attentive, a great listener, intellectual, thoughtful, romantic, spiritual, stands on his beliefs even if someone may believe otherwise, including me (smile), God-fearing, protective, genuine, and an overall amazing man of God and at the time just the type of friend that I needed.

One night on the phone when I was 20 years old, we were having a conversation. I do not recall exactly why, but I built up the courage to tell him that from a young age I was sexually abused by my sister. I had never told anyone else before that day. He said to me that I needed to

"It's All in Me!"

talk to someone about it, he suggested that I talk to my mom. I was hesitant at first because I wasn't sure of how my mom would react.

After building the courage to tell my mother, I found out that she had also been sexually abused by her uncle. This was something that she had never told anyone either. This was a shock to me because my mom had always been very open and shared about her past. This was one thing that she said she wanted to keep us from, so she kept us sheltered specifically from the men in our family. Unknowingly to us, it was a generational curse that would not be stopped until someone spoke up about it. From me opening up about it, my mom was able to open up about it, and then she was able to find out that my sister was being sexually abused by one of our aunts from my grandfather's second marriage and her god sister. From there, not long after that my parents took a trip down south to visit some family of ours and she was led to talk about what we had just discovered about me and told her story. That led to other family members being able to finally tell someone their story of sexual abuse by family members. Had it not been for AJ being a friend and helping me to be comfortable enough to share this deep dark secret that I held on to until I was 20 years old, that generational curse would not have been broken with me.

An amazing woman that I met at an event in 2016 named Natisha Willis, truly changed my perspective on the necessity of friends to obtain true freedom and do the things in life that God has called you to do. One of the things she said that stuck with me is that, "Freedom requires friends." That one small statement took my life into a completely different direction. In her explanation of that statement she said that a Life Coach, therapist, or counselor is a part of those friends that we need to acquire in order to obtain freedom. Prior to that conversation I hadn't even really thought seriously about getting a Life Coach or a therapist. She told us about a program for women to get a Life Coach based on your income. At the time, I was working at an infant/toddler teacher and wasn't making much money, so that was right up my alley. The program she mentioned was, "One to One: Women Coaching Women."

Even after the event it took me a few months to actually take action in order to get a Life Coach. This was because in my family and my culture, those things are seen as unnecessary and taboo. To give you an idea, I went to the event where I met Natisha in July of 2016 and I didn't begin the process to obtain a Life Coach until November of 2016. It only took a few days to receive a phone screening after submitting my application. Then, I was accepted into the program. They originally said it could take a few months. It took a couple of weeks for me to be matched after filling out my profile and other information for them to find me a Life Coach.

My first session with my Life Coach, Sierra Beale, was amazing! We made an instant connection and from there I talked to her every week unless life happened on her end or my end causing us to have to reschedule. The program was only supposed to last six or seven months, but she has worked with me as long as it took for me to obtain the growth that I desired. My last session officially with her was September 18, 2017, but even after completing my official 26 sessions she said will still be there for me anytime I need her. Getting a Life Coach helped me to become comfortable with starting to go to therapy with a Christian Counselor.

I knew that it was time for me to get more help than what a Life Coach could offer when the situation I mentioned earlier with AJ, led to what I considered to be a mental breakdown. I punched a hole in my bedroom wall in a fit of rage, anger, and hurt. During this time, it took my mom almost an hour to console and calm me down. I was shaking, screaming, and crying. Once my mommy was able to calm me down, I was able to look at things for what they were in a clearer state of mind. I realized I needed to go back to therapy. I hadn't been in a therapy session since I attended Coppin State University from 2008-2013. I would go every now and then when I felt like I was losing it. It took a lot for me to tell my mother because I know she isn't very fond of therapists, but I felt as if it was what I needed. I am so glad that I did! It has been wonderful working with Ashley Roberson of *Family Therapy Group, LLC*. She provides Christian Counseling. I found her after doing some research on therapists that take the Maryland State Insurance which made my appointments free. I had my mom who is always an amazing help and guide in my life, my life coach, my business coach/mentor, and other friends and family in my life that I could talk to, but I knew I had more work to do to overcome my past.

I mentioned it a bit earlier, but on July 31, 2017 after much contemplation, and wrestling with God, I finally surrendered to my life's calling of being a full-time minister and entrepreneur. I was so fearful at first, especially when I had to start living off my emergency fund, but God has truly been providing. He allowed me to be able to get the MD State insurance where my doctor's appointments have been free, and my prescriptions have been $1.00. He also made a way for me to get food stamps. I was hesitant to get either of them because I felt as if I was taking advantage of the system, but in the place that I am, and where I feel God has me, both have been necessary. Also, because, I felt like an imposter, helping other people with their financial situation while being on welfare. God reminded me that the provision I was expecting did not come the way I wanted it to, but the State insurance and the food assistance was a part of His provision for me. He also reminded me that my circumstance does not negate my calling. This has been a truly humbling experience for me to truly rely on Him as my provider and source. I was so dependent on my jobs as my source when those were really just a resource from the true Source, which, for me, is God. This entire time God has continued to provide for me.

Let's talk about family in this equation and how my family has been so amazing throughout my entire life! People may say that I am spoiled or that my parents do too much for me at 26 years old, but it has been a true blessing in my journey to freedom and living abundantly.

Minister Jalisa Ray

Growing up we didn't have it all and we still don't, but my mom has always busted her butt to make sure that we have all of what we need and most of what we want. So, now at the age of 26, as I am working on building my businesses and ministry full-time, my mom takes care of me outside of my business expenses and major things for my car. No, I do not pay rent, my car insurance, phone bill, or any other bills. While I was in school for my third B.S. in Natural Health I paid the bill for that along with my student loan bill, which I paid up until December of 2018 just in case. I am very glad I did because it is one less thing I have to worry about while I am focusing on building my businesses and ministry. Prior to this, I did not have a car of my own. I drove my parents wherever they needed to go. In January of 2017, when I was transitioning to a new job, my aunt, Joyce Washington, dropped off a car for me, no car note. It allowed me to take the new job further away making more money. My aunt has been there for every major event in my life. I truly appreciate her and her presence in my life. I don't say it too often, but I appreciate her so much for the example and impression she has made on my life.

These are just a few examples of how my family has been there to support me in my life's journey. I can remember, in 2014, when I pledged Iota Phi Lambda Sorority, Inc. A business and professional women's sorority. At our induction, half of the room was my family there to support me and I had six other line sisters. To this day they still talk about that. My family has been a vital part of my success and progress in life. I do not know where I would be without them.

They say that it takes a village to raise a child. Well, I have needed and had a village all my life in order to get to where I am and to be the person that I am today. I have had tons of mentors, coaches, teachers, friends, family members, sorority sisters, fraternity brothers, co-workers, bosses, counselors, and ministers in my life that have helped to raise and mature me; spiritually, mentally, and physically. Just as many soul ties that took away from me and drained me, I have had

"It's All in Me!"

people in my life to pour into me and replace those things that were attached to me, draining me. My freedom truly came from all of the friends and family that I have had in my life over the years. These are reasons why when I love someone that never goes away even if we lose touch. I have learned so much from people and have had opportunities to teach and share things with people throughout my life that have made all the difference in where I am today. I want to take the time to thank you all again! As I write this, I am in awe of all the people I have had the blessing of knowing, meeting, and connecting with.

Since the age of 10, my church has been a place where I have grown so much and matured spiritually, mentally, and physically. The late Rev. Dr. John Wright was my first pastor at First Baptist Church of Guilford and he played a vital role in my growth as a child. His wife Ida Wright and daughter Dr. Sheila Wright have also played pivotal roles in my life and continue to do so to this day. Pastor Wright's legacy lives on through them. I miss him dearly. God knew what our church needed, and He brought Rev. Dr. Tyrone P. Jones, IV in to take the reins of our church. Pastor Jones and Rev. J have been just what I needed. Many times, Rev. J has prayed over and encouraged me. Sometimes even threatened me in order to get me to where I needed to be in the ministry. Pastor Jones was so patient and caring throughout my process to becoming a licensed minister in May of 2017. My process began back in 2013, but I didn't acknowledge it until 2015. Even without my acknowledgement, he knew and didn't push me until I was clear on my calling and was willing to walk into it. Pastor Jones' spirit and his humility is truly a blessing. He was one of the first people I told the vision to for *Empowerment Unabridged*. He encouraged me to continue to seek God in it and see what He wanted me to do with it. At the time I was caught up in the whole scope of the vision and I was unclear on where to begin so I really didn't do anything with it. I would start and stop on things, but through it all Pastor Jones and Rev. J have been supportive of all of my endeavors in business and ministry. I will be forever grateful to them for all they have been to me and will continue to be to me.

If anyone ever hears me say that I am self-made please remind me that that's not at all the truth. Without all of these people in my life, I do not know where I would be. I am so blessed to have such a vast and supportive network of people that I can count on and they can count on me. I have realized that in relationships it is not just about what someone can do for me. It is about how we can work together to help each other to live out our best lives possible. There were times where I needed help and my family and friends were there for me and there were times where they needed help and I was there for them. I am often looking for opportunities to serve and help my family and friends. That is an area where I definitely need to be more intentional about looking for opportunities to help and give to my family and friends. Sometimes I can be so focused on my life and the things that I have going on, that I do not even think about what my friends and family may need or even think to check up on them. I have used social media as a crutch for that because I say, "Oh, I liked their picture the other day or commented on their status so I'm good." This does not suffice when it comes to building and sustaining strong bonds in relationships. There are times where it is necessary and okay to be focused on your goals and tasks, but there needs to be a healthy balance because as I said, we are not made to do life alone.

On the other hand, I know there are people out there that have unhealthy relationships that may be hindering them. As the Bible says in Proverbs 27:17,

> "Iron sharpens iron, and one person sharpens the wits of another."

"It's All in Me!"

The friends and family that we spend the most time with should be those that sharpen us, and we should be able to sharpen them. The relationship should have reciprocity on both ends. If we are in a place where we have nothing to give we will only be a hindrance to the people closest to us. We all have something to give and we should have willing hearts to give. This goes for the people in your life, they should have something to give to help you as well. If we have people in our lives that only take away from us, then we need to evaluate that relationship. In some cases, they are ungodly soul ties that we need to ask God to help us break and be removed from. We can have strong ties and history with friends, but sometimes in life we grow apart from them and that is okay.

As I said, relationships are for a season, a reason, or a lifetime. Look at that relationship to see what God had for you to get from it. Ask Him if this is a relationship that you need to hold on to or walk away from. In some cases, I had to learn the hard way with this one. Being a person that did not like change, I held on to people that were only draining and distracting me from my purpose. I thought that I would need to stick around so that I could help them. They didn't want the help, and, in the end, I was being hurt more than anything. Most of these types of situations were the intimate relationships that I had been in. I gave a part of myself to them. In some cases, I gave all of myself to them. In these relationships I was being destroyed mentally, physically, and spiritually, but because of soul ties I did not want to walk away. I realized that I idolized the idea of being in a relationship, having someone to call my own, and feeling as if I had their undivided attention. In a way, I made myself an idol in their life, or at least I wanted to be. It was all about what I could get from them, how that person made me feel, and what I wanted that person to do for me. I was in a place where I wanted to be served, but I would only serve them if it benefited me. My service to them was not out of a genuine place of love. I was very manipulative and persuasive. In a lot of cases I used my body in order to do so. God would show me ways out. I would even pray and ask God to show me ways out, but when He showed me I still wouldn't listen.

I would just say, "Maybe that wasn't You God, maybe these were just my thoughts. Please show me another sign." One time in particular there was a guy that I had dealt with for years off and on. All my relationships, the serious ones where the sex had us captivated were off and on. I have not had a long-term consistent relationship without any breakups or breaks. Anyway, I met this guy on Myspace, when it was poppin.' We talked for a while on Myspace and over the phone before finally meeting up and making things official. Things were good at first, but of course being a "church girl" with an extremely overprotective mother, I had to sneak and creep in order for us to be together. Then after I graduated from high school I got more freedom. Spiritually I was torn because I knew that I wasn't supposed to be having sex. But by the time I met him I was in too deep and I had no self-control when it came to sex. It felt good and temporarily filled that void of pain, emptiness, and guilt, so I kept doing it. This was a problem as well because in all my relationships and encounters I just could not be, nor did I want to be, faithful. I cheated on him many times, we would break up, and before we got back together I would tell him that the last time we were together I had cheated on him. He would forgive me, take me back, and we'd do it all over again.

Once I went off to college and started to get back to my relationship with God, I wanted to live right and stop having sex outside of marriage. He was with it sometimes, but other times he really didn't care so it was me trying to abstain by myself while still trying to keep him happy. I prayed to God about whether I should leave him, and I asked Him for a sign. That was not a good idea for a hard-headed person like me. It took a near death car accident and the relationship turning physically abusive, on both ends, for me to finally say enough was enough. Well, sort of… Back in 2013 after a bad breakup and after graduating from college we "reconnected." I hit him up out of curiosity

"It's All in Me!"

and loneliness. He was familiar, and we had history together. Anytime I would go through a break up, nine times out of 10, I would go back to one of my "old faithful" ex boyfriends. So, he came to get me to go spend the weekend with him in VA after we started talking again. Mind you, the last time we reconnected, we stopped talking because some girl text messaged me from his phone telling me not to call or text his phone again and that she was his girlfriend. Put a pin in this situation for later. He explained to me that it was some random girl that took his phone and did that. Apparently, he didn't even know about it. So, I go to spend the weekend with him and we had sex all weekend unprotected. Mind you the whole weekend his phone is blowing up and he's not answering it, but I paid it no mind. Until he left the room without his phone. Can you guess what I did? Yes, I went through it.

The person that kept calling was his girlfriend. He also had videos in his phone of another girl giving him head at work. He had other girls in his phone that he was talking to, as well. We weren't together, so I really couldn't get mad, but I felt dumb because we had unprotected sex. I blamed myself because I was his first and I had brought all of those unfaithful spirits into his life from my past. I carried that guilt for so long, which was another reason why I kept going back. I felt like I had ruined him and turned him into an unfaithful man. Remember what I told you to put a pin in earlier? Well, it happened again. After the weekend was over and he took me back home, we talked for a couple of days. Then I got a text from his girlfriend demanding me not to text or call him anymore. Fool me once, shame on me, fool me twice, shame on you. I had been a fool over and over, him and I both, but this time I really made a decision to be done. God had given me multiple signs to leave Him alone and to get my life together. Majority of the guys I had slept with were unprotected, but by the grace of God, I had only caught Chlamydia once.

I have never been pregnant, as far as I know. There was one time where I think I had a miscarriage, but I don't know for sure. This was in college my freshman year. So, no unplanned pregnancy and no diseases that I couldn't get rid of. All those sex talks, pregnancy scares, waiting for test results, and soul ties didn't stop me from going back time after time to these guys that I had no business being with. I was not being sharpened, nor was I sharpening them. We were only doing each other harm. I realized that I played a major part in the reasons why my relationships were not consistent and why all of them eventually came to an end. The common denominator in all of them was me, so I had to take responsibility. At the end of the day, I could only take responsibility for me and my part in it anyway. I could point the finger and place blame all day, but it wouldn't help me or them. I would have been oblivious, still going in and out of this cycle of unhealthy relationships and ungodly soul ties. This realization is where part of my freedom came from. I could not be free or live abundantly still handling relationships the way that I used to. Not taking responsibility for the outcome of all my relationships. Not just my intimate relationships, but those with friends and family.

God should not have to allow us to be beat up in order for us to let go of the relationships that we are not meant to enter into or hold onto. Evaluate your relationships and the people that you surround yourself with. There are some people that we can call friends, some people we can call associates, and some people we can't call at all. I know some people say that we must be with them in order to help them, but if they are hurting you more than you are helping them, then that is not iron sharpening iron. That is, you making yourself a living sacrifice for a person and not for God the way you should be. Never let someone guilt you into remaining in relationship with someone whom God means for you to release yourself from. It is okay for relationships to end. My cousin once told me, after one of the worst breakups and heartbreaks I had ever experienced that, "The relationship did not end, it was completed." That gave me a whole new perspective on the ending of that relationship and all of my past relationships.

"It's All in Me!"

The season and the reason were accomplished, so it was time to move on. So, think about this when you feel God leading you away from people or when relationships come to an end. It is completed. Thank God for the lessons learned and the growth that you received from it. Even in the worst situations and break ups there was growth and something that you learned from it. Just as healthy relationships play a vital part in our life's journey so do those unhealthy relationships. God works *everything* and *every situation* out for your good. We just have to look at things from this perspective and trust that He has it all under control. If we allow Him to handle things, our lives will be so much easier. As mentioned in the previous chapter, when our relationship with God is in the right place all our other relationships will be in the right place. He will lead and guide our steps and protect us from those relationships that aren't meant for us.

There are some things that I had to do to really get to the place where I am beginning to have a healthy balance in my relationships. As I always say it is a journey not a destination. This is where the self-evaluation comes in. I have had many people tell me that, you are the sum of the five people that you hang around the most. *Do the people you hang around most make you average or extraordinary?* The things that I had to make forward progress in my relationships on my journey to freedom and living abundantly are as follows:

1. **Evaluate where I am in my relationship with God**

    I already talked about this one in the previous chapter. The basis of every healthy relationship should be your relationship with God. He is the Creator of all things and created us for relationship, so He should be the one to show us how to manage and maintain our relationships with other people. If He is not the center of our relationships we end up in messy, unnecessary, and unstable relationships even if certain people are meant to be in our lives. We can cause harm to other people when our relationship with God is not intact. Other people can cause harm to us when their relationship with God is not intact. I have to reiterate this point because I didn't take this into consideration until recent years and really started to see the correlation between how I treat God and how I treat others. I was never truly faithful to God, so I did not see the value in being faithful in my relationships. I did not really take the time to listen when God spoke, so I did not value listening to the people in my life. I listened for my benefit and not for their benefit. I was always tuned into *What's In It For Me* radio. I made it seem as if I was doing or saying things for their benefit, but it was really to see how I could be blessed from being a blessing to someone else. I treated God like Santa Claus and only went to Him mostly when I needed something or when something was terribly wrong. I am still working on the listening to God part because my mind can be so chaotic, and I can be so easily distracted especially when I am praying. I started a routine of praying out loud or journaling my prayers to help limit the distractions. You have to try different things to see what works for you.

2. Evaluate the people that you spend most of your time with

I'm sure that you've heard the phrase, "Birds of a feather, flock together." This is so true, and people sometimes deny it, but we are heavily influenced by the people we spend the most time around. We begin talking like them, using the same mannerisms, picking up their habits, going along with the things that they go along with, and becoming connected to them through spiritual and mental soul ties. It is important to really be mindful of the people we spend a lot of time with because it is so easy to become connected to someone through a soul tie. Ask yourself questions, especially about the areas in which you struggle. How do the people I spend the most time with handle these areas of their life? For me, my weight and my health has been a challenge all of my life. Many years have gone by where I have had this same goal weight.

"It's All in Me!"

I would start programs, start diets, start exercising, Zumba, yoga, Zija, and Noni, but none of it would stick. I once watched a webinar hosted by Courtney Sanders, "Think & Grow Chick," where she talked about our habits and the things that we say we want to do, but never really get around to doing it. Or we start something as a New Year's resolution, but half way into March we quit. She taught about the three factors that contribute to this phenomenon most of us know so well.

These factors are knowledge, beliefs, and values.

She said that if you have this goal or dream that you can never seem to stick with or never seem to reach it is because one or all these aspects are not in proper alignment. You may need some additional knowledge or information about the goal that you are trying to accomplish. You may need to evaluate and change your beliefs around this goal you are trying to accomplish, or you may have some conflicting values that you need to reconcile in order to accomplish this goal. I realized that when it comes to anything with my health, it is my values. I have the knowledge because I have been studying holistic health since 2011. Prior to that, I knew that there had to be a better way because the conventional way of medicine didn't work for me. I also have a degree in Natural Health and have been mentored by a Doctor of Natural Medicine/Naturopathic Doctor since 2012. So, knowledge is not my issue. Belief is also not my issue. I believe that it is necessary for me to be healthy and be at a healthy weight. I believe that it is possible. I believe that the knowledge I have is true. I believe that I can achieve these goals of being healthy. So, belief is not my issue. My biggest challenge is my values. Growing up and even living at home now the values that I was raised with around food, health, and weight do not coincide with my beliefs and my knowledge.

I have values where food is for comfort and it brings my family together, my father loves going to buffets so we grew up going very often and we still do to this day. Fried and fast foods, frozen and processed foods are what we grew up on. I value them to the extent of the memories that I have around them. I have appreciation for these foods because at one point in my life they were all we could afford. It was not about the nutritional value of the food it was about survival. We didn't have the knowledge or resources when I was growing up to make better choices. This was all I knew until I grew up and began to study. Still living at home with people, who to an extent still have conflicting values from the ones that I am training to live by has made the transition more difficult. My family has come a long way over the years and they take heed to a lot of the things that I share with them about health and weight, but we still have work to do in these areas.

All my life I was told conflicting stories. I was bullied by some people about my weight, but others that loved and cared about me, told me that my weight was fine and that I didn't need to lose any. These conflicting stories growing up have created conflicting values in my life right now where I struggle to really be consistent with eating healthy and working out. I know the benefits of it, but part of me still feels like I am fine the way that I am. I get sucked into this comparison trap when I get around people that are smaller than I am, or bigger than I am, or have more health challenges than I do. It makes it hard for me to stay focused on my goals and desires around my weight. These conflicting stories also come from thinking about who sets the standard for a healthy weight for me? What does that even really mean? The normal BMI chart doesn't fit my body type or my makeup, so that for me never made sense for me to try to aspire to. So, I have had to set and define it for myself. I know my "why" around wanting to lose the weight and be healthier. I want to be the best example possible for the people that I am called to help, and part of that example is being healthy.

What does being healthy mean? Who defines what healthy is? Is it the absence of dis-ease and discomfort? I have acne, chin hair, and am "obese" according to the standard BMI scale. Does that mean I am unhealthy? Does that mean that I am healthy? I haven't really come to a

"It's All in Me!"

conclusion about what it means to be healthy or at a healthy weight, so on my journey I am working to reconcile these values.

The other part of my "why" is so that I can be at a healthy weight for when I get married and start having children. I don't want to be uncomfortable during my pregnancy and sick throughout it. I do not want my children to have birth defects, be miscarried, or become stillbirths because I was unhealthy prior to and during my pregnancy. I want to be able to have an easy and natural birth. I want to be able to be confident and comfortable around my husband naked. I want to be able to bounce back right after having my children. I want to be active and healthy when my grandchildren come along. I do not want to have to battle with Alzheimer's, diabetes, cancer, or high blood pressure as I get older like my family members have. These things are a part of why I want it, but my values around it still has been a hindrance to me. It really has nothing to do with willpower or self-discipline. It has everything to do with my knowledge, beliefs, and values. I have had to ask myself the question, *"Do you value you?"* This has been difficult for me to answer because for so long I did not. It wasn't just about the foods that I ate, but all the drugs I did, all the guys that I slept around with unprotected, all the times I put myself in harm's way, all the times I got stupid drunk and should have had alcohol poisoning. The things showed me that I did not value myself. I had created a habit of devaluing myself. In order to come to a place where I can truly say that I value me and that I am worth living a healthy lifestyle, and maintaining a healthy weight, I have had to struggle and fight.

I am making progress in this area every day. It is a journey not a destination. So, ask yourself, *what are your beliefs, what knowledge do you have, and what values do you have around the people in your life and the unhealthy habits that you have held onto for so long?* Do not just evaluate your knowledge, beliefs, and values, evaluate your close friends and families, as well. Things will begin to make much more sense as to why you haven't been able to reach and maintain those goals and dreams you have had year after year. Do not just give up on it because you haven't been able to do it. There are millions of other ways to accomplish it that you have yet to try. Be open to the plan changing but keep the goal the same.

3. Evaluate the level of reciprocity in your relationships and your motives behind what you bring to the relationship

Is there a level of give and take to your relationships? Are you able to receive in your relationships? Are you able to give in your relationships? Why do you give the way that you give in your relationships? In my intimate relationships I realized that so many people took things from me, my innocence, my dignity, my pride, my confidence, my trust, and my freedom. It made me feel as if they owed me something or that I owed them something. I had given myself to so many others, I felt that I had no choice, but to continue to do so. It was a crazy way of thinking, but it fueled my motives for why I handled relationships the way that I did. I had this idea that I would, "get them before they got me." I hurt a lot of people this way and ended up being hurt a lot as well. I would dig a ditch for them and have to end up digging another one for myself. I wasn't able to do and receive things out of love when it came to my intimate relationships. I didn't know what true love was, which is why I keep saying that the foundation of relationships should be God. God is love and without love, the relationship will fail. As I said, I would do things in hopes to get the other person to do things for me or to get them to act or behave in a certain way. It wasn't really for them, it was for me.

I thought that in order for me to keep a man and keep them from cheating on me, I had to have sex with them. If I didn't I knew that someone else would, so I did it to keep him happy and make him stay. In the back of my mind, I assumed that he would cheat anyway, so I made sure to cheat before he could. I *always* had a backup plan. Even if it was just a friend or an ex on standby that I rarely talked to. When things went south with one, I was quickly on to the next one. I perpetuated this cycle pretty much all my life. Seeing how my mom was treated by my dad and she was as faithful to him as they come, I made a vow to myself that I would never let a man make a fool of me the way she did. I knew how to give, and I knew how to receive, but my motives were all jacked up. When you look at your relationships ask yourself those questions I mentioned at the beginning of this section. To get the most benefit out of your relationships, evaluation must occur. There must be some level of intentionality for relationships to grow and flourish.

They are like any other living thing. For them to grow they need nourishment and attention. Without that, they will fade away and eventually die. I didn't take the time to really evaluate this until I wrote this book. I always wondered why my relationships didn't work out. Not just with guys, but with family members and friends. I had not been truly intentional about any of them. I hadn't taken the time to evaluate them for what they are and what I need to do to make sure that the relationship is getting what it needs to grow and flourish. If you are like me and you consider yourself to be a seasonal friend, then it is time to evaluate some things. Even if you are not it is still time to evaluate some things. Don't just hold on to a relationship because you have history with someone. Iron sharpens iron, if neither of you are being sharpened, it may be time to let the relationship go.

Reflection Questions:

1. How would you rate your relationship with God on a scale of 1-5? Why?

---

2. How would you rate your relationship with others on a scale of 1-5? Why?

3. Are there any ungodly soul-ties you have not dealt with yet? To who or what?

4. What are some things you can do to deal with these soul-ties now?

"It's All in Me!"

5. Which of these, your values, knowledge, or beliefs hinder your relationships most? Why?

_____
_____
_____
_____

6. What can you do to keep the one you chose from hindering your relationships?

_____
_____
_____
_____

My Prayer for You:

Father God,

Your daughter or son is seeking to know You better. They are seeking to understand You better. They are seeking the right relationships and the right people in their lives. They have had people in their lives that hurt, used, and abused them. They have had people in their lives that loved and supported them. They have been in relationships that resulted in ungodly soul ties. They are seeking freedom from these ungodly soul ties. Please lead them in what they need to do to be freed from the soul ties once and for all. Let them be able to move on without trust issues or defense mechanisms. Let them move forward with the expectation of loving and healthy relationships. Let them move forward with all that they need to be a healthy and whole person in all their relationships. Let them be able to let go of the people that they may not want to but are not meant to continue with them on their journey to freedom and living abundantly. Let them have the strength to say no, to remove and block people from their lives that mean them no good. Remind them that they are worthy of love and being loved. Show them that they are capable of loving someone. Show them how to obtain and maintain healthy relationships. Make it clear and make it plain where there may be confusion and blurred lines in their relationships. Show them where they are with You and where You have for them to be. Thank You in advance for the healthy and flourishing relationships they will have from this day forward. Thank You for the healing they will experience from this day forward. Thank You for the freedom they will experience from this day forward. Thank You for putting things in place in their life so that they will never be connected to an ungodly soul tie from this day forward. Thank You God for the support village you have and will have around them. Thank You that they will not have to do this thing called life alone. Thank You for the people You will send their way when they feel lonely or alone. Thank You for creating them for relationships with You and with others. Thank You for their life and the calling You've placed on their life. Have Your way in their life and their relationships. Thank You for working everything out for their good. Thank You for the new relationships that will be established. You are truly worthy to be praised. I know that You will do exceedingly and abundantly above all that I or them could ask or think. All the glory belongs to You!

In Jesus' name I pray,

Amen

Chapter 3: Forgiveness/Forgetfulness

Forgiving and forgetting has been the hardest part of my journey to freedom and living abundantly. The hardest person for me to forgive has been my future husband first and then myself. Maybe they were neck and neck. I knew that I needed to forgive myself when it came to the things that I did in my past. As I mentioned before, I have had almost 40 physical sexual partners. That was a hard pill for me to swallow once I sat down and counted one day. After going through a cycle of off and on relationships, always having a "ram in the bush," and moving quickly on to the next one and the next one, those soul ties began to add up. I felt so ashamed and guilty. I knew that God had forgiven me, but I just couldn't forgive myself. Especially when I was still in bondage to ungodly soul ties some willingly and some unwillingly. Like a dog, I continued to go back to my vomit. I would "fall," cry and pray to God, asking for forgiveness and fake repent. I say *fake repent* because I didn't truly turn away from that relationship or those sins that I easily found myself running back to. My repentance was not genuine.

Genuine repentance is when you turn away from the sin or object of sin never to return. You decide to sever the tie to it and cut off all opportunities to go back. It is genuine repentance when you renew your mind to think differently about the sin you once desired. I always left the door cracked open "just in case." Just in case I wasn't satisfied with what God was doing or how He was doing it. I could go back to what was comfortable and familiar. Part of the reason I had a tough time forgiving myself was because I knew I really wasn't done with the sin that provided instant gratification. I was so caught up in it, I would say that I was addicted. Addicted to the high that the sex and the attention gave me. Addicted to the pain that I was feeling from everything from my past. These things had become a part of my identity and letting them go made me feel like I was losing a part of me. Going

Minister Jalisa Ray

to a Christian counselor helped me to realize this. Also, I really hadn't forgiven my future husband the way I thought I had. My counselor asked me to write a letter to the woman that I didn't know about. One of the most important lessons that I have learned in my many journeys through life. Here's the letter that I wrote:

> *You don't know me, and I don't know you, but there is a message in my mess that I want to share with you. You, like me, have probably been hurt many times and you may even nurture the pain the way I did. Anything that you nurture will grow, and you will grow attached to it. When I had to let go of my hurt it caused me fear and anxiety because I felt as if I was losing a part of me, a part of my identity. That's not who I am nor who I believe you are. You are healed, you are whole, and there is purpose for your hurt/pain. The purpose of your pain is to make you stronger and to make you realize you can't do this alone. Even though it may seem like God doesn't love you or seem like he doesn't care, He absolutely does more than you will ever know! You may not understand right now how a loving God could allow someone He loves to go through so much pain but think about His Only Son whom He allowed to be tortured, beaten, and killed. His pain was for a purpose bigger than his human self. There is a purpose for your pain as well. When you can let it go and take responsibility for you and forgive those who hurt you, [including you], the purpose will begin to show. It doesn't excuse what they did to you, but it frees you from carrying the pain and the burden of it. As hard as it may be, don't take it personal because hurt people hurt people. Show them how to*

"It's All in Me!"

heal... Future generations will thank you! (8/18/17 8:38pm)

The day that I realized that pain was one of my addictions helped me on my journey to true healing and freedom from it. It gave me permission to forgive myself and others. It was for my own good. I'm sure you've heard this saying before, "Unforgiveness is like drinking poison and expecting the other person to die." In the case of others this makes sense, but when it comes to you, when you don't forgive, in this sense it's suicide because you won't forgive yourself. When you don't forgive yourself even knowing that God has forgiven you and sent your sins into the sea of forgetfulness, you tell Him that His forgiveness is not enough. That it is not enough to truly cover and take care of your sins. You are telling Jesus that His blood was not enough to wash away your sins. So, forgive yourself! Let go of the things that you did in your past and even the things you have the desires to do in the present or future that you know aren't the right things to do. You are forgiven for your past, present, and future. That is one of the many gifts of salvation and coming to Christ. Now if you're not saved then you can receive this forgiveness right now. Ask God into your heart and truly mean it. You too can enjoy the freedom of forgiveness.

As I said earlier, the other person it was hardest for me to forgive was my future husband. It wasn't until recently that I realized this going through a few sessions of Christian Counseling by myself and pre-marital counseling with him. So, here's our story.

We met on the campus of Coppin State University around my second semester as a Freshman. I had gotten to college and gotten more freedom. I mentioned earlier that my mom is very over-protective, so a lot of the things that other teenagers my age were able to do I wasn't. I found a way to still do those things without my mother knowing.

Terrible, I know! Once I got to college and I was, "on my own," I took full advantage of it. I partied, drank, smoked, slept around with three guys and had a one-night stand. All the while still having a boyfriend that lived near DC that I mentioned earlier. In passing, AJ and I became friends because we had mutual friends that we hung out with. We played dominoes and spades all night some nights.

My first personal encounter with him, as he says, was me stealing his money. We were in the lounge of one of the dorms at Coppin playing spades or dominoes. People wanted stuff from 7-Eleven so those that weren't playing were asked to go. It was me and a few of my female friends. We walked about two miles to the 7-Eleven. AJ had given me his money for his stuff. On the way back from 7-Eleven it began to rain so I was upset! At the time I still had a perm so getting my hair wet was not a good look! So as my tip for the trip and getting wet in the rain I kept his change. He asked me for it and I told him that it was my tip. He was upset but he wouldn't really say that he was upset. I remember sitting next to him and he hit my thigh with the side of his fist in conversation. I knew he was upset, but I didn't care. I was upset that I had gotten my hair wet in the rain. From there we still only spoke in passing when we would see each other. A few months later, one of the guys I had slept with, his friend, told me that AJ asked him for my number, so we could talk more as friends. I said it was fine. I thought it was weird, but I was like, 'Okay sure, why not?' From there we started to text just about every day. Even though at the time, I still had a boyfriend and a side guy, who was also AJ's acquaintance.

I would say that I had an on-campus boyfriend and an off-campus boyfriend. AJ and I became very close over the next three years or so. He was like my best friend. He was there every time I got my feelings hurt. He was there when I was in an abusive relationship with my ex off campus. He was there the third instance when I was raped. He was there when I was scammed out of $800. He was there for my 18th birthday and bought me three big bottles of alcohol. He was there when I needed help moving on and off campus and even moving from one place to another at home. He was there for family functions and I was there for his family functions. For me, things got too close because, he wasn't my type. I ignored his advances until June 23, 2011, not long after officially breaking up with my off-campus boyfriend, when I decided to "give him a chance." He knew all my dirt, he knew my past, my weaknesses, and my strengths. He knew me better than any other guy I had dealt with.

    About six months in, something told me to go through his phone. I was extremely hesitant because as they say, "If you go looking for something, you'll find it." I had trust issues, but he really had never given me any reason not to trust him. I did it anyway. I found out that he had an online relationship with a girl from back home that was going on for about a year and a half. All the while he was telling me I was the only one he wanted to be with, there was no one else, and all that good stuff. On the other hand, he was telling her all the things he wanted to do to her. I was devastated! I could not believe that this man that pursued me for three almost four years would really do this. I had been hurt so many times before, but this one hurt a little bit differently because I thought things would be different with him. I had let my guard down and I was really in a place where I was working on living my life for God. By this time, I had an ungodly soul-tie to him because I coerced him into having sex with me after he was celibate for four years. I told him things like he was gay or that he didn't really love me because he had never tried to have sex with me. I equated sex with love. So, this was another blow to my already fragile heart. I was so angry and hurt! I told him what I saw, and we argued outside late at night in front of the dorms. He stayed calm and didn't allow me cursing him out and saying very disrespectful things get to him. He even stood in front of me and invited me to punch him in the face so that we could move past it. I wasn't having it. I went to my dorm crying and he followed me.

Minister Jalisa Ray

I called one of my exes from back home who was like my best friend. We were in each other's lives for years by that time and we were there for each other through our different phases of life. We had slept together a few times, but we were still able to just be friends. During our conversation, he asked me a simple question after I told him everything that happened, he said to me, "Do you love him? If you love him then work it out, if not leave him alone."

I loved AJ and I was in love with him, so I decided to stick it out. Remember I said that I already had trust issues that I hadn't dealt with properly? It wasn't a good idea to stay in that condition after he broke my trust, but I did. Instead of me, "getting him before he got me," it turned into a, "I'm going to get you back," situation unintentionally. I say unintentionally because I wasn't seeking someone out to cheat on him with. I did allow it to happen though. I was already hurt and didn't trust him. I should have left him alone instead of cheating back on him. After telling him what happened, a day or two later, that I had cheated, he decided that we would stay together and work it out. Then a year later he broke up with me because he couldn't handle the fact that I cheated. Crazy right?

After a while it turned into a "tit for tat" situation. I don't think that was our intention but looking back at it now that's what it was. We kept allowing other people to come between us, so we ended up having an off and on relationship as well. The entire time he never officially got with anyone else, but he made emotional and spiritual soul ties with people during that time. According to him though he never cheated or even pursued anyone else because he hadn't had sex with anyone. Yet he had sex driven conversations, conversations about marriage, and other incidents of inappropriate things being said, on both ends, with quite a few females and these are just the one that I know about. He got hip to the fact that I would check his phone from time to time, so he would delete messages and e-mails. I checked e-ver-ry-thing!

"It's All in Me!"

Does this sound like a healthy relationship to you? Not at all! Yes, we had a lot of good times, even great times, but the entire time we weren't doing things God's way. We were straddling the fence and doing some things His way and other things our way. During us going back and forth, I continued my promiscuous behavior and jumping from relationship to relationship and situationship to situationship. You may be asking what in the world a situationship is. A situationship is a relationship without the boyfriend/girlfriend title that includes all of the benefits of the boyfriend/girlfriend relationship. I met one guy on an app and the night we met in person we had sex, the next time we saw each other we had sex unprotected.

When I tell you, God was looking out for me! My God!

I was chasing this high that I couldn't get enough of. I was looking for love in all the wrong places. All the while God was trying to get my attention, but I didn't want to listen. I kept going to church, but the church was not fully in me. I wanted to still have the best of both worlds.

Literally, my future husband and I have been through hell and back! If I could go back I don't think I would do anything different because it has and will make our relationship/marriage stronger and built to last. We have been through things that people wouldn't even think about coming back to each other after, but every time we ended up back together. God confirmed for both of us that we were meant to be together, but we didn't want things on His terms, we wanted them on ours. Had we been obedient we would have been married by now. We forfeited God's perfect will for his permissive will. His perfect will occurs when we are obedient. His permissive will occurs when we decide to do things our own way but in the end God will still have His way. We had both been hurt by each other and other people. We were two hurt people continuing to hurt each other. Through all of this I thought I had forgiven him once we reconnected back in February of 2017. The 25th to be exact. On a drunk night celebrating my birthday after not drinking or getting drunk for a couple of years, I did my normal routine of drunk calling/texting my exes. Two in particular. AJ was one of them. AJ and I hadn't been in contact for five months or more. We had gotten into a heated argument that turned into him putting me out of his house. Things almost turned physical. Afterwards, I was going through a season of "singleness." Not completely because I still had one guy I was dealing with heavily, but we weren't together. We tried it, but it didn't work, so we were just close friends. For a few months I wasn't dealing with anyone. I felt God was calling me to a true season of singleness where I would just focus on Him and be committed to Him. After getting drunk and getting back in touch with both of my exes that all went out the window. The night I got drunk my other ex came over and we had unprotected sex. This was the ex, who was like a best friend at the time, that I called when AJ cheated the very first time. Mind you during this time I was going through my Minister in Training process. I was still trying to live my life straddling the fence. Prior to that it had been almost a year that I was abstinent. I was devastated that I had made those bad decisions. I felt as if I was headed back to becoming the old me. It goes to show you how one "small sin" can lead to bigger sins.

Sin is sin and it is not to be played with. If you give the enemy an inch, he will do what he can to take your life. His purpose is to kill, steal, and destroy. It all started with "just one drink" on my actual birthday on February 18, 2017 and it all went downhill from there. This "one drink" led to me being in an unintentional love triangle being confused as to who I wanted to be with. In between February and May of this year I was having sex with both AJ and my other ex. There was one day in particular where I had sex with both of them. I called that "thot behavior." Here's the kicker: AJ proposed to me April 7, 2017. I had cheated again, but in my mind because it was on a night that we had gotten into a fight and I called myself "breaking up with him," I didn't consider it that. He didn't feel the same way because according

"It's All in Me!"

to him, even when I was with other guys I was still his and he was still mine. He never tried to really be in a relationship with anyone else. Every time we broke up he would come back or take me back without hesitation. The night I "broke up" with AJ while we were engaged I ran to my ex crying and angry because I ASSumed that my future husband was with another woman. He was right there to comfort me in more ways than one. After that my ex was talking about marriage because I had told him I was done with my future husband. That unfaithful roaming spirit was high and exalted. I was playing games. I knew it, but because I had feelings for and soul ties to both of them it was hard for me to let it go. We all ended up hurt.

So, here I am again trying to forgive myself, seek forgiveness from God, and seek forgiveness from my future husband. All the while ignoring the fact that I had unforgiveness in my heart towards him. I was caught up on what I had done and didn't stop to acknowledge the hurt that I felt and the unforgiveness I was nurturing. I had a very nasty attitude and disposition towards my future husband. I blamed it on just being heated in the moment when we would argue but we started to have, in my perception, more arguments than conversations. All I saw were his flaws, mess ups, mistakes, and imperfections. When we would argue I would be very rude, disrespectful, curse him out, and highlight all the things he was doing and had done wrong. Going through counseling and journaling helped me to see that the root of it all was unforgiveness. I had to learn to switch my focus to the positive things. I had to acknowledge my unforgiveness and the fact that I hadn't dealt with all of the hurts from my past. He was the object of my wrath. I was taking everything that was done to me out on him every chance I got. It took for me to say that we had to take a step back in order for me to really focus on God and my relationship with Him in order for our future marriage to work. Going into it with all those toxic behaviors and attitudes would have probably ended in divorce. Every chance I got I had this habit of walking away when things didn't go my way. A situation that didn't go my way was the cause of me calling off the engagement even after cheating on him with my ex and him staying. I made a selfish decision, but it was for both of our good.

The way that God started me on this journey to genuine forgiveness and further preparation for marriage was a 21-day absolute fast. I had completed five days earlier in the year of 2017 but even that wasn't preparation enough to do 21 days. I originally planned to do about 10 days, but God had another plan. Once the engagement was "officially off," I began this new journey to forgiveness not just of myself, but forgiveness of my future husband and all the people who had hurt me that I was blaming him for.

Those 21 days were a series of ups and downs. I was not just being spiritually and mentally purged, but physically purged as well. I experienced a healing crisis in which my acne on my face flared up so bad my whole face hurt for almost a week. A healing crisis is defined as a normal process that toxic individuals will often encounter on their path to getting well. The medical term for healing crisis is the "Herxheimer Reaction." I was a toxic individual in more ways than one. During the 21 days God called me to season of preparation for Him to continue to purge, cleanse and make me whole. It was confirmed to me a few times that this was what I needed to do to truly be in a place where I could say that my future husband will find me as a wife and not just a girlfriend. I want to be a wife when I get married, and not just be married. Originally it was supposed to be a season of complete singleness but that wasn't the case because I promised myself to AJ in marriage. He was not my boyfriend I could break up with, he was my fiancée. God brought the Scripture to my attention about making promises. He also reminded me of how serious an engagement is, it's not just something you could "call off" on a whim. An engagement is a legally binding contract. I'll explain later how we officially got back together. The terms of the season of preparation

"It's All in Me!"

were that we would not talk at all until the 18th of every month and we wouldn't see each other at all.

Things are hard because we make them hard by being hard headed and disobedient. Some may say that these terms are radical or drastic, but to get to where God wants me to be and become who He has for me to be, I have to be drastic and radical. I was drastic and radical about living in sin, so I decided to be drastic and radical about living for God. Most people including my future husband doesn't agree with it but I know that it is what God had called me to do, so I was obedient. During the first month, I saw how God moved and worked in my life. I truly surrendered my life to Him instead of trying to do things on my own and in my own strength. It was one of the easiest and stress-free months of my life. I learned to just be with Him and didn't have to try to get things done. I saw how God was doing things in my life. He doesn't really need our help. This book is a perfect example of that. He blessed me every day to sit and write for an hour without dealing with interruptions or roadblocks. This was one of the easiest and most enjoyable things I have ever done. I would previously overthink things and try to get ahead of myself, but now I just allowed God to flow through me to get the words on these pages. He has already written my story from beginning to end it's only right for Him to be the one to do this. God provided all the resources and tools I needed to get his done. Including my business coach/mentor who was with me every step of the way!

Now let's talk about this forgetting thing… This one for me was pretty easy to a certain extent. It is a very complicated thing for even me to understand. Some things I forget easily other things I don't. I haven't really been able to pinpoint categories or certain types of things that I forget easily and the things that I don't. Being a survivor of so much trauma I learned to easily forget things. Sometimes this is to my advantage other times it is frustrating. I do not remember a lot of the good things that happened in my past and only glimpses of the dreadful things that happened. The sexual abuse in my childhood for the most part I blocked out. I feel like I am crazy sometimes because I don't remember everything. Part of me says that it didn't happen, but the parts that I do remember always let me know that it was real. When it comes to even my high school or undergraduate years I do not remember specifics about what happened. It was God that lead me through writing this book because a lot of the things I didn't recall until He brought them to my remembrance. As I said, sometimes it is to my benefit because for some survivors of abuse, or rape, have to deal with reliving those things on the regular basis. They are able to remember the smell of the room, the paint on the walls, and the color of the shirt they were wearing in detail about the days, times, and instances of these tragic events in their lives. It also has benefited my significant others to an extent.

When they do something, and I allow myself to get mad I do not stay mad long because I forget what happened depending on exactly what it is. It is hard to explain, I think I just have an extremely selective memory. I can remember certain things but not all things like some people who can remember dates, times, and where they were. On the other hand, in my case because those precious and positive memories that some people can recall I'm unable to most times unless someone jogs my memory vividly. Even sometimes then I still don't remember. My memory is very complicated. I thought about all of the courses I have taken in college with all three degrees. If someone gave me a test on most of those things, I would probably fail. It sometimes makes me feel less than, but when it comes to forgiveness, forgetting is necessary. It can also be the hardest part of forgiveness. Just like our sins go into the Sea of Forgetfulness, the things that people do or say to you should as well.

We cannot say that we truly forgive someone, but every time we have a disagreement with them we bring what they did back up. When I would do this, it showed me that I hadn't truly forgiven my

"It's All in Me!"

future husband. Every single time we would get into a heated argument, if I didn't say it, the thought about things he did in the past would come to mind. It would fuel the wildfire that was my mouth. It was awful. I do not know how he has continued to put up with me all these years. He was the only person that I would allow to make me mad enough to curse. Notice I said allow. No one can make you feel a certain type of way, you choose how you're going to feel based off of their action or inaction. You choose how you're going to respond to something. Back to the forgetting, I hear people say all the time, "I'll forgive you, but I won't forget." *Why not? What is remembering it going to do for you?* Just like harboring unforgiveness harms you more than the other person, so does unforgetfulness. Yes, that is a word according to my spell checker.

Holding on to what someone did or said instead of just forgetting about it, only hurts you. For me, it only added fuel to an already raging fire. I chose intentionally not to forget those things. Other things like, what I wore to church last Sunday I forget as soon as the next day hits. The day after a test I forget everything that I stayed up all those nights studying. I would say that I have a selective memory sometimes intentionally, sometimes unintentionally. Writing this book helped me figure that out. I used to really beat myself up about it. I really would think that something was wrong with me, but it's just the way things have been for me. There are probably exercises that I could do to remember things, but somethings are better left forgotten. I have still been able to heal and forgive in addition to forgetting. I have had to forget people, places, and things to truly move on in my life. For you it could be totally different as I said you might remember everything. It's time for you to be intentional about forgetting some things to truly be free and get the healing that you deserve. If you choose to remember, let it be from a perspective of victor, not victim. Let it be for the use of helping someone else. You deserve to heal, you deserve to be whole, you deserve to live life to the fullest. Part of that for you is forgiving and forgetting. They go hand in hand. Yes, it may be difficult, especially for those of us who have had trust issues. I understand completely! You do not want to be made a fool of repeatedly. That is why discernment and being led by God into and out of relationships is important.

I cannot say what your situation will be and what God will or won't do for you, only He knows. I can only speak from experience. The people in my life that were meant to be, the friends people called me dumb for staying friends with, eventually were, "killed with kindness and love." I was able to win them over with love. I did not allow the things they did that hurt me to keep me from showing them the love they needed. That is what it all comes back to, love. I am constantly reminded of a question when I allow my future husband to get on my nerves. Do you love him? Every time and for everyone the answer should be, yes. We are all worth loving and we are all lovable. Nothing you or I have done in our past, present or future can make us unlovable, thanks to the grace of God and His Son's sacrifice. You and I are worthy of unconditional love and so are all of the people you feel are unforgivable.

God loves them the same way He loves you. Jesus died for them the same way He died for you. He forgave all their sins just like He forgave all of yours. There is no excuse for the things that they did of course, but the price has been paid for them. The highest price of them all. The price that you're trying to make them pay is nothing compared to the price that Jesus paid. *Was the price He paid not enough? Do you feel they owe you more than they owe Jesus?* Stop trying to be the one who punishes people and let God do it. Trust that God will take care of you and serve justice to those that hurt you. Forgive and, "fugget about it!" Remember this:

"It's All in Me!"

Deuteronomy 32:35 New King James Version (NKJV)

35 *Vengeance is Mine, and recompense; Their foot shall slip in due time; For the day of their calamity is at hand, And the things to come hasten upon them.'*

Romans 12:17-19 New King James Version (NKJV)

17 *Repay no one evil for evil. Have regard for good things in the sight of all men. 18 If it is possible, as much as depends on you, live peaceably with all men. 19 Beloved, do not avenge yourselves, but rather give place to wrath; for it is written, "Vengeance is Mine, I will repay,"[a] says the Lord.*

Reflection Questions:

1. How would you rate your ability and willingness to forgive on a scale of 1-5? Why?

_____
_____
_____
_____

2. What are some things that have happened to you that you felt were/are unforgivable?

_____

3. Who are some people that you need to forgive?

4. What are some things that you think you can do to forgive them now?

My Prayer for you:

Father God,

The person reading this prayer has been hurt a few times or many. In some ways that only you know. I want to thank you for forgiving them

"It's All in Me!"

and for sending Your Son to die for their sins. I pray that they were able to read this chapter of this book and that they are truly set free from the things that have had them bound in a place of unforgiveness and unforgetfulness. They deserve to truly be free, healed, and whole. In You, they are just that. Help them not to take things personally, but to always be reminded that hurt people hurt people and to be able to help some of the hurting people that hurt them to heal. Let them be in a place where the vivid memories that haunt them cease and that they can use it as a part of their testimony for their healing and others. I speak forgiveness/forgetfulness into their spirits, souls, and bodies right now in the name of Jesus. That they forgive themselves, forgive others, and most importantly that they forgive You. A lot of people don't want to talk about it, but some people have not forgiven You. They blame You for allowing those tragedies to happen in their lives. They blame You for allowing their loved one to die. They blame You for that miscarriage they had after trying and wanting a child for so long. They blame You for their parents not wanting them. They blame You for allowing that person to abuse them. They blame You for allowing it all. But in a world full of sin and the fact that You have given us free will, we know that You are not the one to blame. I speak that they will be able to see the true purpose in their pain and that they will begin to rejoice in it and truly count it ALL joy. I know that it won't be comfortable to do it but help them to truly surrender and turn all those things that they have been holding against other people over to you. That they can move on and be set free from those things in wholeness and peace. Give them peace of mind knowing that we all get what we deserve here or on the other side. Give them the strength that they need in you to stand up against those negative thoughts and feelings around those tragedies that occurred in their lives. You have it all under control. You know their exact situation and the things that have them bound. So today I speak freedom over their lives, that they will no longer be bound by unforgiveness and unforgetfulness. Let them forgive and forget what is

Minister Jalisa Ray

necessary. Have Your way in their lives. I thank You in advance for working it all out. It's already done!

In Jesus' name I pray.

Amen!

Chapter 4: Feeding My Mind

"Feed your mind, starve the doubt." - Tony Fleming

This quote is what one of my past mentors would tell me all the time. He emphasized how important it was to overcome the fear and doubt that comes when you are an entrepreneur. He emphasized to read the Word, of course, but also books about the things that are required of entrepreneurs. The stories of people who have successfully become entrepreneurs and maintained their businesses, and general topics about personal growth and self-development. He emphasized that personal growth and self-development is just as important, if not more important than the information and knowledge that is acquired from formal education. In this journey of reading, listening to, and watching content that is considered personal growth and self-development, I have learned and held onto more than in my 20+ years of formal education. There are life lessons that I have had the privilege of learning first from the Word of God and second from the personal growth and self-development materials. I have sat under millionaire and billionaire mentors and coaches for health, finances, business building, money, confidence, and speaking. I absolutely would not be this far in my journey without them and the information and knowledge that I have acquired. It was my mindset outside of these principles and ways of life that have kept me from being more successful. Another quote that I learned in this journey of what some call "self-education." *"You cannot change the situation you are in with the same mindset that got you there."* -Brian Beane This reminds me so much of a Scripture that has played a pivotal role in this journey of "self-education." That Scripture is Romans 12:2. Romans 12:2 has been a guidepost for my life. I have always been a reader. I learned to read at a very early age. My life has been transformed by the constant renewal of my mind through reading. Romans 12:2 states this,

Minister Jalisa Ray

2 *And be not conformed to this world but be transformed by the renewing of [your] mind, that ye may prove what [is] the good and acceptable and perfect will of God.*

Instead of watching TV sometimes, I would rather read books growing up. Instead of going outside to play sometimes, I would rather read books. I was so fascinated by the stories that I encountered while reading. When I read even to this day, the content and stories come alive. My love for reading has truly been a blessing! I am absolutely sure that without it, I would not be who I am today. I would not have as much wisdom and knowledge that I have. Of course, growing up as a preacher's daughter and pastor's granddaughter, I was heavily influenced by Word more often than most children my age as well. I had a children's Bible, Bible story books, and watched Veggie Tales. I even went to a Christian school for elementary where we memorized Scriptures, the books of the Bible, and had courses specifically about The Bible. Every day I was constantly having my mind renewed by the Word of God. This foundation ensured that even though I did stray very far away, I came back to my foundation and what I know as the truth for my life. I never really realized how much the pieces of my life's puzzle came together and made so much sense, until I began to write this book, talk to my mom about my life and my childhood, and really reflect on it all. My last degree program required tons of reading and writing. From my childhood, that love for reading and writing translated into my diligence to complete a program that most people my age has not and would not have been willing or able to complete.

The Dean of my program told me that he was very surprised that I had gotten as far as I had in my program at the time we spoke, because the average age range for the people who start and complete the program are around 36-53. He said very few people my age starts the program, let alone finish it. I ended up finishing a five-year degree program a month shy of three years. Without this discipline and habit that was bred into me from an early age, I probably would not have been able to finish the degree program either. The program required me to read through entire textbooks and complete or create different assignments based off the chapters. Some of the final number of pages for the course assignments were 100+ pages of content that I had to create and write. This program also prepared me for writing this book now that I am thinking about it. I built the discipline to just sit and write for extended periods of time. To sit and research, read, and write for extended periods of time which is necessary as well in order for me to write this book. I had research about my life and some of the things that I put in this book. Of course, because I have a challenging time remembering things about my life, as well as in some cases where certain Scriptures are in the Bible, research was necessary for me to write this book.

Romans 12:2 is one of the Scriptures I will never forget. One, because as I said it has been a guidepost for my life. Two, because it was one of the Scriptures I needed to memorize while going through my process to become a member of my sorority, Alpha Nu Omega Sorority, Inc. in Spring of 2011. This Scripture has followed me all my life. I have overcome so much and so many tactics of the enemy because of my habit of continuously allowing my mind to be renewed by the Word of God and other materials I feed it. It has been a continual process and journey. In some cases, my beliefs and the information that I had was not helpful, but a hindrance. Some of the things that I believed based off my experiences and what I read kept me in bondage to certain behaviors and habits. Without renewing my mind, I would not be writing this book. I would not be on my journey to freedom, to holistic health and wealth, to becoming a wife and mother, or on my journey as a full-time entrepreneur. Renewing my mind has been one of the major keys to all my success.

I make sure every day to at least read one Scripture daily if not in a Bible plan, from an app, or from an email subscription. I get into the Word daily. Throughout the years, I have changed and transitioned how I interact with the Word, but nonetheless I have kept up a daily habit of at least reading something out of it daily. At one point in my life, for years, I would pick a Scripture, write it out, and journal about what it meant to me and how I could apply it to my life. As I got older, I started to doubt that I was really learning anything from it since I couldn't quote Scriptures off the top of my head. What I am about to tell you, most people do not even know about me even as open as I am about my life. I have a deep-rooted insecurity about my interaction and depth of knowledge about the Word. I am hesitant to even say it, but here goes.

When it comes to the Word of God, my insecurity about my depth of knowledge about it comes from my challenge with remembering specifically where a certain Scripture or passage of Scripture is in the Bible. I even doubted that I was called to become a licensed minister because of this. Outside of when I was a child and going through my process for Alpha Nu Omega Sorority, Inc. my ability to memorize and retain the location of a Scripture has pretty much been non-existent. I even tried to use the tools and tactics of memorization that I used while I was going through my process for $AN\Omega$. That still has not worked. I am reminded that I know what the Word says and that I live out what the Word says and that's what's most important. But for me, that hasn't been enough. I want to be able to quote Scriptures verbatim and include their location in the Word. I want to be able to tell people who may not read the Word or know the Word where they can go to find Scriptures relating to their situations in life. I sometimes envy or compare myself to people in that matter. Especially people of other religions that know their Holy Teachings

"It's All in Me!"

front to back like Muslims, Mormons, and Jehovah's Witnesses. I feel intimidated by them, their work, and desire to convert people of other faiths. In the midst of my insecurity, I am also reminded of my story and experiences with God. My story and my experiences with God are what draw people to me. My story and my experiences with God are what this book is about, and for now that is enough. That doesn't stop me from trying diverse ways to retain this information, but it doesn't bother me as much as it used to because of this revelation. I do not have to allow the enemy to make me feel insecure about what God has called me to do and the way He has called me to do it.

I do not have to feel insecure about not knowing where a specific Scripture or Scripture passage comes from. When it comes to this, Google has been my best friend. I put in a portion of the Scripture into Google and the Scripture reference comes right up. In that case, I am grateful for technology and the ability to have access to information instantaneously. It has been a true blessing in me overcoming and dealing with this insecurity.

This habit of feeding my mind has led me to a place where I strictly monitor or limit the intake of mainstream media. I have not had a television in my room for about seven or eight years now. My parents even bought me a purple one to go in my room while I was in college and I gave it to my future husband to put in his room. I was so disinterested by the quality of the shows that was on television and the way that African-Americans have been portrayed that it turned me off to it. In addition to that, my mentors saying repeatedly, that I shouldn't be watching people fulfill their dreams and their purpose if I'm not fulfilling my own. I watch it every now and then, when I am spending time with other people or I will watch a documentary or an interesting movie on Netflix. Outside of that television is not a major pastime or hobby of mine. Majority of Americans spend a major portion of their life watching television. Here are some statistics from this year as of

Minister Jalisa Ray

May 2017 published by BLS American Time Use Survey, A.C. Nielsen Co.:

Total Use of Television	Data
Average time spent watching television (U.S.)	5:11 hours
White	5:02
Black	7:12
Hispanic	4:35
Asian	3:14
Years the average person will have spent watching TV	9 years
Family Television Statistics	
Percentage of households that possess at least one television	99 %
Number of TV sets in the average U.S. household	2.24
Percentage of U.S. homes with three or more TV sets	65 %
Percentage of Americans that regularly watch television while eating dinner	67 %
Percentage of Americans who pay for cable TV	56 %
Number of videos rented daily in the U.S.	6 million
Percentage of Americans who say they watch too much TV	49 %

"It's All in Me!"

Child Television Statistics	
Number of minutes per week that the average child watches television	1,480
Percent of 4-6 year-olds who, when asked to choose between watching TV and spending time with their fathers, preferred television	54%
Hours per year the average American youth spends in school	900 hours
Hours per year the average American youth watches television	1,200
Number of violent acts seen on TV by age 18	150,000
Number of 30 second TV commercials seen in a year by an average child	16,000

These statistics to me, say a lot. African Americans spend the most time watching television and in my opinion have the most difficulty getting ahead. The television shows that are about us that we watch most are shows that promote, drugs, sex, violence, homosexuality, and so many other things that portray us in a negative light. Let alone watching the news where the major highlights are of us being killed, killing each other, fighting, living on the streets, acting foolish in public places, and living off welfare. These images that we are constantly allowing into our minds do affect us whether we want to admit it or not. The things that we constantly feed our minds influence our lives. There is no denying it. If you research the wealthy and their daily habits I can almost guarantee you that 99% of them watch little to no tv. I could be overestimating, but from the people I have read about, watched, and listened to that are wealthy, they do not watch television *especially* not the news. The majority of what is on the news is doom and gloom. There are more positive and encouraging things going on in the world, but television and entertainment streams focus on pumping out CNN or constant negative news. The reason is because that's what sells and that's what people prefer to watch. To me that is very sad. These are reasons why our world looks the way that it does today. The media is constantly using the negative images and content to keep people trapped in bondage to the things of this world. Constantly showing and advertising the things that will keep you from living up to your fullest potential.

Have you ever fasted from media for a time just to see how much of an effect it has on your life? I once read an article about loneliness and how a remedy for loneliness is less social media and technology. It was ironically after a conversation I was having with my mother about the amount of technology my family and I are accustomed to. I have a laptop, cell phone, two tablets, two cameras, access to Wi-Fi, a Bluetooth printer, another printer, *Netflix*, *Pure Flix*, a firestick, and cable. Even with all of these things, I still feel lonely sometimes. This article I once read said that loneliness is becoming deadlier than obesity. They have begun to call it the "loneliness epidemic." To me it is interesting and a bit insane that we have so many ways of being "connected," but we have the highest instances of loneliness than ever before. Here's a portion of an article that talked about the reasoning behind less social media and technology being a remedy for loneliness. This article is by Dr. Axe which is entitled, "Loneliness: A Worse Killer than Obesity + What to Do About It."

"It's All in Me!"

"Occasional feelings of loneliness are not problematic if you do something to relieve yourself of lonely feelings. According to psychologist John Cacioppo, Ph.D., from the University of Chicago, "Loneliness is actually an evolutionary adaptation that should spur us to get back to socializing, a state in which we are happier and safer." (7) Now let's look at some of the best natural ways to combat feelings of loneliness and get to a much more enjoyable state of mind and being.

You may enjoy social media at times, but at other times, maybe you've wondered or even searched the Internet for: "Do I have an obsession with Facebook?" Technology and social media can be quite addicting and time-consuming. On the positive side, you are able to keep in touch and maybe even form relationships with people all over the world. On the negative side, you may find you're spending a lot less time connecting with people in person, getting outdoors, exercising, being creative and practicing other habits on a regular basis that help decrease feelings of loneliness.

A study published in 2017 in the American Journal of Preventive

Medicine found that heavy use of social media platforms, including Facebook, Instagram, Snapchat and Instagram, was correlated with feelings of social isolation. Specifically, this study looked at 1,787 adults in the United States between the ages of 19 and 32 and found that people who spent more than two hours each day on social media had double the likelihood of feeling socially isolated and lonely. Researchers also found that the people visiting social media most often (58 visits or greater each week) were more than three times as likely to feel socially isolated compared to people who visited less than nine times each week. (8, 9)

It's also really important to consider the effects of social media and technology use on children when it comes to loneliness. A U.K.-wide study conducted by the Royal Society for Public Health released in May 2017 revealed that imaged-focused Instagram "is considered the social media platform most likely to cause young people to feel depressed, anxious and lonely." Snapchat came in second followed by Facebook, Twitter and YouTube. (10)

It's totally up to you what social media you choose to take part in (or allow your children to take part in), but reducing

"It's All in Me!"

your time using technology in general can make a huge positive impact on your life and actually help with feelings of loneliness. An idea to remember is "disconnect to connect," which means being intentional about being present in the moment, especially when you are spending time with loved ones or doing something you enjoy. Turn off your phone when you can or put it on silent. There will always be time to check a text or an email, but you can't get cherished moments back and you can't really enjoy what you're doing when you're not fully there."

Feeding our minds and spirits includes the technology we decide to use and the amount and quality of social media and other forms of media we choose to partake in. We are constantly bombarded subliminally and intentionally with certain images, energy waves, and messages that have a major impact on our minds and entire beings. We must be more intentional about what we allow into our gates. These gates being our senses and our mind/heart. There are even Scriptures that talk about it. One in particular that comes to mind is Proverbs 4:23 which states,

> *"Above all else, guard your heart, for everything you do flows from it."*

Minister Jalisa Ray

Since everything we do flows from our mind/heart, we need to be mindful about everything that we allow to come in contact with it. That includes television, certain people we follow on social media, certain videos we watch on YouTube, certain music we listen to, and certain movies we watch. What we feed our mind, flows to our heart, and our actions begin to show exactly what we are feeding our minds. You will only be able to cover it up or hide it for so long. One day when you stub your toe, someone cuts you off, or some tragedy occurs in your life, what you have allowed to have access to your heart will show. *How have you been guarding your heart, if at all?* The enemy has slowly desensitized us to things that would not have been acceptable previously. Certain things that would not have been normal are now considered normal. Sex outside of marriage is now the norm and it is even accepted on television shows and movies. It is considered in some cases rated, "PG-13."

Whereas, back in the day there weren't even kissing scenes in mainstream media. It didn't go from no kissing to full blown sex scenes overnight. It gradually went from allowing kisses on the cheek, to kisses on the lips, to tongue kissing, to touching inappropriately, to scenes that led up to just before the sex scene and then fade out, to soft porn scenes where they made sure body parts were covered, to full blown sex scenes where you see body parts. This is how the enemy has worked with all sins. He has worked through media and technology to desensitize us to sin. We wonder why the world is in such a disarray, it has a lot to do with what we are feeding our minds and our children's minds. We think it is cute when children know all the lyrics to rap songs but fail to pay attention to what the lyrics are saying. What these lyrics and songs are feeding their minds, hearts, and spirits. We must be especially careful with what we feed the minds of children because they are like sponges! They suck up and hold on to anything that you pour into them. I cannot stand to hear parents speaking negative things at and about their children. It really bothers me because those things affect

"It's All in Me!"

them tremendously later. When they get older and play into being those negative things they've always been called, then it's an even bigger problem. But those are the seeds they've planted into them from an early age. Or when they begin to curse at them, their teacher, or other people they want to chastise them when they've been cursing them out all their life.

It is no longer a "do as I say and not as I do" generation. We must show the generations behind us the way to live, talk, and interact with each other. Otherwise, our bad actions and media will show them. You may feel as if it is okay because they are young, and they won't remember, but they will, and they do. Just as you wouldn't give your child a cigarette, a bottle of alcohol, a blunt of marijuana, or a pornography magazine, do not subject them to vulgar and derogatory language, music, television, and media. Those things open their minds, spirits, and hearts to things that they should not be opened up to as an adult, let alone a child. We do so much damage to our children by the words we speak to them and the things that we allow them to be exposed to knowingly and unknowingly. But now, you don't have an excuse. This goes for your children and your inner child. There are so many positive things to read, listen to, watch, say, and expose ourselves to.

This is how we begin to experience another level of true freedom and living abundantly. We free ourselves from the values and beliefs of the world. We are no longer willingly bombarded with the negativity and nastiness that media pushes on us all day every day. This was the reason why I asked about fasting from it, because you will see the difference that it makes in your life when you go without it. You will begin to see how much you are addicted to it as well and how much control it has over your life. When you feel lost when you go without technology and media you will see. We are so addicted to technology and media that it has also become the norm. To be out with family and everyone is looking down at their phone or electronic device instead of just being with each other. Trust me when I tell you, you are not alone. This is something that I must be mindful of myself. I realized that I use Facebook to fill the void of not having a male to talk to on the regular basis at night before bed, like I have a majority of my life. I made a conscious decision to be obedient to what God asked me to do. Yet, like any other time where I was supposed to fill those voids with Him, I chose other things. I had days where I stayed up until 5am on Facebook just because.

Facebook helped me to fight the urge to call someone else, but I didn't choose to call on God during those times I felt lonely or weak. This has been what social media, media, and technology has been for a lot of us. We have turned it into an idol. Instead of us being more intentional about feeding our minds positive things and the things of God, we choose things of the world.

We choose television, movies, Netflix, Hulu, Facebook, Snapchat, and Twitter to fill the voids that God, His Word and the fellowship with His people should fill. I am not saying that every aspect of these things is wrong, but the majority of what is produced and advertised to us on these outlets are not things that we should indulge in let alone become addicted to. So much so, that we put these things before God. Instead of listening to the sermon we're scrolling down our news feed. Instead of waking up in the morning and praying, we choose to check our phones to see who's called, sent a text, tagged us in something on social media, or what everyone else is doing with their life. Instead of taking the time to acknowledge God and allow Him to feed our minds, hearts, and spirits before we are bombarded with things of this world. This is how we guard our hearts and essentially feed our minds what it needs to get through each day. By starting out acknowledging God and thanking Him for waking you up, asking Him to equip you for the day with your daily bread, opening His Word to see what He has to say to you, and sitting in silence to listen for His voice, you feed your mind the nourishment that it needs to grow and

"It's All in Me!"

produce your true purpose. When we feed our minds things of this world, we produce things of this world. We produce the ways of this world. We produce not walking in purpose or walking our own path. We produce the duplication of someone else. We produce children that perpetuate this same cycle. It is so important to be mindful of what we feed our minds.

Had I not been in a place where I was willing to not only continue my formal education, but also my "self-education," I would still be lost. I would still be walking the path of bondage and not the path of freedom. As stated, I still deal with the addiction to my phone and social media, but because I am aware of it and can give it over to God, He can work on me with it. He can free me from it. There are healthy and productive ways to use media and technology. We just must find the balance.

We must ask ourselves, *"Is the way that I am using this resource that God has provided me with, glorifying Him or me?"* Or, *"Is the way that I am using this resource showing that I love Him, others, and myself or is it showing that I hate Him, others, and myself?"* I know that this is a bit extreme with the hate side, but it is literally that serious. It is a matter of life and death. The things that we partake in and post on our social media accounts can either lead someone to life or lead someone to death. Everything that we allow into our minds makes a difference. Every little thing makes a difference. I know this may be a hard pill to swallow or you may be asking, "Okay. Yes, I have these challenges or maybe even addictions. What do I do about it?" Here are some of the things that I did to make the shift from merely existing to living abundantly and from a mindset of bondage to a mindset of freedom.

Minister Jalisa Ray

1. **Evaluate and make note of what you tell yourself on the daily basis for at least a week**

When I had to really pay attention to my thoughts and the things that I told myself on the daily basis I realized just how toxic my thoughts and my thought processes were. To change our thoughts to be more positive and productive we must first become aware of them. Becoming aware of our thoughts will also help us to evaluate the quality of the media and other things we are feeding our minds. I hear this quote all the time by Bob Proctor as it pertains to the Law of Attraction, "thoughts become things." The things that we see in our lives start as thoughts. When things begin to appear in my life that I do not want I have to check in with my thoughts and the things that I have been feeding my mind or not. When I do not make intentional effort to read my Word daily or indulge in other positive information I see the difference in my life, demeanor and attitude. A way to evaluate this is to also journal about your day and go back and read to see your perception of the things that occurred in that day or in that week. When I indulge in media or social media that has derogatory scenes or words I see the difference in my thoughts and actions. I am more prone to fall into sin because I have fed my flesh for it to grow. There is a story that I have heard about two wolves. Here's an article I found around it and the story of the two wolves:

> Our negative thoughts can create anxiety, anger, resentment, jealousy—an array of emotions. Negative thinking is normal. However, if this way of thinking becomes incessant, it can lead to depression and self-destructive behavior like addictions, derailing us from what we want most in life. At minimum,

"It's All in Me!"

negative thinking saps our energy, erodes our self-confidence and can put us in a bad mood. Certainly, many would agree that our thoughts come and go so quickly that it seems impossible to notice them, but with awareness and an attitude of self-compassion, we can redirect our negative thoughts to more positive ones.

Two Wolves is a Cherokee Indian legend and illustrates the most important battle of our lives – the one between our good and bad thoughts. Here is how the story goes:

An old Cherokee is teaching his grandson about life. "A fight is going on inside me," he said to the boy.

"It is a terrible fight and it is between two wolves. One is evil – he is anger, envy, sorrow, regret, greed, arrogance, self-pity, guilt, resentment, inferiority, lies, false pride, superiority, and ego." He continued, "The other is good – he is joy, peace, love, hope, serenity, humility, kindness, benevolence, empathy, generosity, truth, compassion, and faith. The same fight is going on inside you – and inside every other person, too."

Minister Jalisa Ray

The grandson thought about it for a minute and then asked his grandfather, "Which wolf will win?"

The old Cherokee simply replied, "The one you feed."

Our thoughts can be our own worst enemy. That is, if we let them. Think about how you may be "feeding" your negative thoughts by allowing them to rule your mind. Next time you have a negative thought, catch it and ask yourself, "What is this thought doing for me?" You will find that the answer is that all they are doing is disempowering you. You can immediately feel more empowered by focusing on something good in your life and cultivate the practice of gratitude.

We can create greater peace, confidence and a more positive outlook by learning how to manage our thoughts. After all, this battle can be won because we have the power of choice!

Which wolf are you feeding? Remember, you always have a choice.

So again, I ask, which wolf are *you* feeding? It makes all the difference in our battle with our old and new self that God created us

"It's All in Me!"

to be. I kept falling into the same old, same old sin until I realized that I had to be more intentional about the part of me I had been feeding. I couldn't watch the same thing the world was watching. I couldn't listen to the same stuff the world was listening to. I couldn't read the same stuff the world was reading. I couldn't follow the same people the world was following. I had to do something different to get different results. Some may say that this is radical, but if we can be radical with our interactions with and ways of the world, we can be radical for Christ. It is necessary!

2. **Evaluate and make note of what forms of media you take in and how much time you spend doing so daily for at least a week**

Having to take the time to evaluate what I was taking in via social media, media, books, articles, and movies was a challenging task. Even though for years I have not really watched television, I still find myself caught up in shows that I know do not feed my spirit but feed my flesh when I am watching television with other people. I do this instead of me being the party pooper and saying that I don't want to watch it. I do it for the sake of spending time with my loved ones. This is how I got caught up in Power, Jessica Jones, and The Haves and Have Nots. I rarely watch them, but when I do it matters. I would have urges to have sex, watch pornography, or masturbate. My dreams also became very sexual when I would watch those shows. As I said before everything that we do and every decision that we make counts. It makes a difference in whether our spirit or our flesh grows. To truly overcome sin, we need to be more intentional about feeding our spirit instead of feeding our flesh.

One weekend I let myself be so busy with everything that I didn't make the time to sit with God and meditate on His Word like I normally do during the week. I found my self snapping at my brother more than usual. When he said to me, "Why do you keep yelling at me?" I realized that I had been missing out on nourishing my spirit, so my flesh was taking over. Even if you don't indulge in mainstream media, but you slack off in indulging in the Word and time with God it will make a difference in the way you behave. I use a tracker app on my phone to track my activities, mainly the time I spend on social media. You can use it for music, television, reading, social media and anything else that you feel may be impacting your thoughts and actions. This way you will see how much time you spend on these things. Make sure to differentiate the positive from the negative influences. Remember this if it gets a bit confusing.

Does this glorify God or glorify man, (which includes yourself)? That way it shouldn't be as difficult to differentiate between the two. There are some things that may sit on the line for you, if so the best thing to do is to either avoid it or put it in the negative category. When you evaluate the time spent on these different activities, then go further and evaluate the quality of the day or week you had. *Were you very negative, catching attitudes with people, arguing with your significant other, or falling into sin more frequently?* From there, pick certain things to fast from and see if things improve or stay the same. I was told at an early age by a minister of music that I couldn't listen to secular music because of how it impacted me spiritually. As I got older, I didn't listen and from sometimes I still don't listen, but I am more aware of how it affects me because I know this. This can be the same for you, so this exercise can make a world of difference for how you show up in the world.

3. **Plan time into your day to read, study, and meditate on the Word to make it a habit and part of your daily routine. Start out with 10-15 minutes if you feel as if you don't have enough time to do so or get up earlier.**

"It's All in Me!"

This is something that I believe should be done more than 10-15 minutes a day, but in order to give people somewhere to start without feeling overwhelmed I say 10-15 minutes to begin with. Six months to one year from now, you shouldn't still be spending 10-15 minutes with God. Just like we're supposed to tithe our talents and treasures to God, we should be tithing our time to God. 10% of your time that you are awake is about 1.6 hours if you sleep 8 hours a day. So, if you do an hour in the morning and an hour in the evening, or even break it up into 15 or 30 minute sessions throughout the day, it will make a huge difference in your life and your relationship with Christ. He has so much He wants to show us and tell us, but we are too busy doing, that we miss out on the time of just being with Him. It doesn't even have to be a lot. Sometimes just sitting for 15 minutes just to listen to Him will make a world of difference in your day and the strength of your spirit man. I have a bunch of different ways that I make sure to get my Word in and my time with God.

I have about two or three different email subscriptions that send me devotionals. I have the Abide app, the Daily Devotions app, the YouVersion Bible app, and the First 5 app that all send me notifications throughout the day to remind me to get into and meditate on His Word. I even have an app that reminds me to pray. I don't always follow that one, but I am working on improving my prayer life by praying out loud or journaling my prayer to start my day because I found that I am less distracted and don't end up falling back to sleep. This is something that I just started recently so I am seeing how it goes. There are some mornings where I don't feel like opening my mouth or going to my desk to write, but once I do, it helps me to focus and get ready to start my day. You must find tools, resources, and tactics that work for you to make sure that you make spending time with God a priority. This is the most essential part of feeding your mind. Be intentional about it.

4. Research and identify books and other positive materials to partake in daily for at least 10-15 minutes to make it a part of your daily routine.

Okay, so, when it comes to this strategy you have to be very selective on whose advice you take. This is the reason why having a foundation and a relationship with God is so important. Personal growth and self-development material is great for inspiration, motivation, and encouragement, but no one can or should be able to tell you the best decision for your life. Partaking in this material should not dictate the directions for your life. People can only tell you from their experiences and partially from the experiences of others. They really don't know exactly what someone else goes through because they are not living their life for them. Even if they are close family members or friends. For you, you have to use what God tells you and what His Word tells you, which are the same, to direct your path in life. The things that you read or advice that you receive from this material should not contradict what God has told you. It should not take you in a different direction than the direction that God is taking you. There are a lot of useful information and resources out there, but all of them are not of God.

Do your best to line up the principles you learn from these materials with the Word of God. If you get confused or can't find exactly where it correlates with Scripture ask yourself, *"Who does this glorify, God, myself, or someone else?"* Most of the time you'll be able to get clarity from answering this question. If not, then don't hesitate to ask God if this correlates with His Word and His Will for your life. He cares about every single detail of your life. If He knows the number of hairs on your head, He cares about the principles and information you are taking in. This is how I have had many of what I call, "virtual mentors/coaches," people that I have never worked with personally or even met in person, but I have read their books, taken a course, watched videos, and found other ways to follow them and learn from their wealth of knowledge and experience. Especially when it comes to finances and business because these are the areas where I have had the most challenging times. If there is an area where you struggle there are all sorts of materials on that area and how other people have overcome in those areas.

5. **Research and contact a mentor, therapist, life coach, or someone you can talk to about the negative thoughts you have and the addictions you may have identified, when it comes to mainstream media, social media, or anything else you may have discovered during your time of self-evaluation.**

At one point in my life, I had probably 8-10 mentors/coaches pouring into me. All of them had good, even great intentions, for helping and seeing me go further in life. The problem was that they had differing opinions, so this naturally caused confusion because I wasn't in a place where I was able to discern what was for me to do and what was not. It became very frustrating. So, I decided to step back from all of them to just hear from God about what He wanted me to do. I took a long hiatus from getting coaching or mentoring and just took the time to be and do things. To learn and apply things. I eventually came to a better place of stability and confidence in who God created me to be and do. The Bible talks about having wise counsel. In Proverbs 11:14 it says,

> *"Where there is no wise guidance, the nation falls, but in the multitude of counselors there is victory."*

Minister Jalisa Ray

I used to think that this Scripture meant that I personally needed a multitude of counselors, what it really it means is that the nation should have a multitude of counselors. Even in the Bible days, there was a need for counselors and wise guidance. Anyone having too many counselors would cause them confusion the same way it did for me. I experienced this in 2017 while working with a Life Coach, a Business coach/mentor, and a premarital counselor. I was also following other people on social media, attended their webinars, participated in their Facebook groups, subscribed to their e-mail list, and followed them on YouTube. I had the opportunity to have a discovery call with two coaches that I follow to learn more about their programs and what they have to offer for business coaching. As I mentioned, I already have a business coach, but it was a free opportunity to talk to someone else doing what I am in the process of doing and who have more experience, so I took full advantage of it. Can you guess where this left me? Not confused this time, but with more options that I did not really need. I had been working with my business coach to focus on writing this book and preparing for the speaking and teaching engagements that I had coming up.

Things had not worked out as well as I would have liked them to with one-on-one wealth coaching, but I continued to push forward with it. September 1, 2017, I got my first paid coaching client. It was a step in the right direction, but had I taken the advice of the other coaches I would have gotten off track. Not to say that their advice wasn't great and that I won't use it in the future, but right now this book and these upcoming speaking engagements, teaching engagements, and workshops are where my focus will be. I am not focused on making money. I am focused on making a difference, an impact. By doing things that way, I know the money will come regardless. Yes, I still have financial goals, but I am not stressed out about them. I was stressed and worried prior to really surrendering things over to God. I have had regular discussions with my therapist and business coach about the things that I used to fill the void that only God is supposed to fill. My

"It's All in Me!"

business coach encouraged me to limit or take a break from social media for a time so that I could break the bonds it had on me. I've done it before, but it was necessary to do again to get more clarity and direction for my business and my relationship with my fiancée.

Even if you don't want to talk to a counselor, therapist, life coach or anyone yet, journaling to God is a wonderful thing to do. God knows exactly what we are thinking and how we feel so that we can be completely honest in our writing. It gives us the chance to get it all out and to go back later. It allows us to see how God worked on that situation and the feelings we had around it. When you find someone you can trust to talk to about your life's challenges, you will have another resource to help you on your journey to freedom and living abundantly. Again, with this, make sure that you are doing your research and making sure that the things that the people you connect with in this manner are in alignment with what God has told you. If you feel as though the things they are telling you are contrary to what God is telling or has told you, then you will need to move on and find someone else. Wise counsel can also be a Pastor or a minister at your church. I had a spiritual mentor who was a minister at my church.

She prayed with me, I could talk to her, and she would hold me accountable to my prayer life and studying the Word. I could talk to her about the spiritual battles I was dealing with. For some mentors, coaches, and counselors you may outgrow them or naturally be separated from them just like a friend. Some are for seasons, reasons, or lifetimes. Don't feel as though you have to stick with one person forever. There are levels to your growth and maturity that require new levels of help. Even people who may seem like they have it all together and are wealthy and successful still have counselors that give them wise counsel in order for them to maintain their status. They seem to have it all together because they have a team of people behind them making sure that is the case. Like my "virtual mentor" Natisha Willis says, *"Freedom requires friends."* Other people especially who are trained and have the experience can help you to see things from a different point of view than you would not have seen on your own.

My Life Coach through the One-to-One Woman Life Coaching program was a phenomenal help and at the time of publication, I had one more session left with her prior to the completion of this publication. I was sad about it. I talked to her every week give or take. The amount of growth she has helped me to achieve has been amazing. She really showed me the confidence I never knew I had. She empowered me to come to conclusions on my own by asking questions. She is one of the reasons why I decided to become a holistic wealth coach. Some of the things she empowered me to do was to say "no" to people, things, and opportunities that were not beneficial to me. This translated into me being able to say "no" to job opportunities that came my way after making the decision to never go back to Corporate America. She supported my decisions and made sure that I fully thought through them to ensure that I was making the best decisions. She is also a believer so that helped tremendously!

My business coach as I said earlier is a major reason why I have gotten so far in this book writing process. She gives me the accountability and the no-nonsense coaching that has been life changing when it comes to the progress that I have made in this current stage of my entrepreneurial career. Having someone to listen to me and be able to listen to myself speak about my challenges helps me to come to better conclusions about my decisions. Talking to God first as my source to know whether someone in my life is wise counsel or not is a huge part of it. There were some people that I came across and asked for help, or mentorship, that were not in alignment with God. He removed them from my life one way or another. When relationships naturally dissolve, that is part of what you should seek God about. *Was it for the purposes of the season ending, the reason being accomplished or were you unevenly yoked?* Yes, you can be unevenly yoked with a mentor, coach, or counselor. This does not only go for intimate relationships. You can

"It's All in Me!"

be unevenly yoked in any kind of relationship. As I mentioned in an earlier chapter, there are times when I had to pray to be released from the ungodly soul ties with who I thought to be wise counsel. I was caught up in the things that they were teaching me, the things that they accomplished, and wanting my life to look like theirs. This is another important aspect of working with a coach, mentor, or counselor. You should not begin to model your life after theirs or begin to covet their life. The purpose of their relationships is to help you along *your* path. Their life is their life and their story is their story. Model your life after Christ and Christ alone.

Reflection Questions:

1. How would you rate the quality of your self-talk on the daily basis on a scale of 1-5? Why?

___

___

___

___

2. How would you rate the quality of the media you fill your mind with on the daily basis on a scale of 1-5? Why?

___

___

___

___

3. How would you rate the amount of time you spend on feeding your mind positive material on a scale of 1-5? Why?

4. What are some things that you could limit or eliminate from the media and material you fill your mind with daily?

"It's All in Me!"

My Prayer for you:

Father God,

I want to thank you for the person reading this. For them taking the time to invest in themselves and their journey to freedom. For them recognizing that they have or are experiencing some bondage in their life. For their desire to be free and free indeed. We know that whom the Son sets free is free indeed. I thank You that they have had a renewed mind in reading this and about the things that they feed their spirit, heart, and soul with. I thank You that their desire to be filled with You has been refreshed or even ignited today. I thank You that You can sweep out all that is not like You within them so that from this day forward they truly walk in the new creature you created them to be. That they will truly walk and reflect your image. Father God someone was exposed to things unlike you from a very young age and those images still replay in their mind. God, I ask that you stop and destroy those images and the replays of those experiences right now in the name of Jesus. I ask that You cover their mind in the blood of Jesus. I rebuke any attack on their mind that the enemy has set or is even working on them as we speak. The enemy has no power in their life, in their mind, or anything dealing with their life or their future. I speak victory in their life over every test or trial that may come their way. I speak peace of mind during a storm. I speak the easy yoke and the light burden in their life. Let them not carry unnecessary weight and let them be reminded that You are always there to carry the load with them. God remove all the old ways of thinking and old beliefs that do not serve them and do not glorify you. If there is anyone in their life that is causing confusion, help them recognize it and act accordingly. Lead, guide and direct their steps as they seek You through Your Word and as they seek out wise counsel. Let

Minister Jalisa Ray

the wise counsel for them be in line with You so that the messages and the information they give are in line with Your Will and the Word that You've already given them for their life. Have Your Way! I speak true freedom in their mind and that they continuously feed the righteous side so that their spirit man will be stronger than their flesh. Let them walk and worship in spirit and in truth. Thank You God in advance for hearing and answering this prayer because I know that it is already done.

In Jesus' mighty and matchless name, I pray,

Amen!

Chapter 5: Find My Own Path

Finding my own path has been one of the hardest yet most rewarding journeys of my life. I have always been one to be, what some would consider a rebel. I was never really one to follow the crowd, I was the one normally leading whether in a positive or negative direction. I have always been influential and persuasive. I was the first to do a lot of things among my friends and family.

The first to "lose my virginity." This is in quotations because as I mentioned I was sexually abused by my sister and did sexual acts with a couple of my boy cousins before officially "having sex" at the age of 13. After being exposed and really engulfed in darkness, I had to find my own path to the light. I ran from God and ran back to Him so many times in my life, but all the while He was there looking out for me. The night I lost my virginity it was to a guy I barely knew and that I had lied to about my age. I told him I was 16 and, at the time, he was 19 years old and what I considered to be an alcoholic. I wasn't a drinker at the time. He offered me something to drink, but I declined. I had made a "pact" with a few friends of mine about us losing our virginity around the same time. At 13 years old, also being the youngest of my friends because I was a grade level ahead. I was the first to do it. It was one of the worst experiences of my life. I regretted it as soon as he started. I was a "G" though. I didn't cry, but it hurt like heck! I said another word at the time when I was explaining it to my cousins who I was hanging with that day to get out of the house and my friends later. I bled and afterwards I was walking funny because of the pain. Not long after, I stopped hearing from him and he no longer worked in the mall where I met him. So, basically, my "first time" was a one-night stand. It took me a short while, I would say almost six months or more to even attempt to have sex again.

After the second time, I guess that was when Pandora's Box was opened in a way because after that there was no stopping me. I managed to go from guy to guy being passed around like a piece of meat. Guys that were related to each other, guys that knew each other, guys I knew for years, and guys I barely knew. Looking back, I wasn't paying attention to how many there were. I was chasing the feeling, chasing the high to fill this void or this black hole that had become my soul. The more I fed it, the more it grew. Things became so perverted at one point, I was even addicted to watching and masturbating to gay pornography and bestiality.

The enemy is not going to stop at "a little sin," there are levels to the ways he will come in and turn your life upside down and have you doing, thinking, and saying things that you never would have imagined. Especially when it comes to sex, the levels of perversion are literally out of this world. I was so ashamed of where I had gone, and I refused to tell anyone. I haven't told anyone until writing it in this book about the type of pornography that I was addicted to. I was so disgusted with myself. I did all of this, but still stayed in church and in service. No one really knew what I was doing when I wasn't in the church except for my friends and cousins that I did my dirt with. I was able to "successfully" live a double life.

This chapter was tough for me to write because it required me to expose my entire past. I wasn't really caught up or didn't experience any sort of writer's block until I got to this chapter. As I said, I was in relationship after relationship and situationship after situationship all the while ignoring the one relationship that truly mattered. The relationship that should have been above all other relationships. Until I really acknowledged who God was and who He was to me, I was on a path that wasn't the true path He intended for me. I was on my own path built upon my own decisions, my own wisdom, and my own understanding. I was on the path that led to destruction. For me to find my own path I had to turn from following the enemy and who he was telling me I was and turn to following God. I had to switch my focus from those thoughts of, "You always go back to having sex, drinking, cursing, lying, or living in sin, so stop trying to live right." Or the thoughts that would plague my mind of not being worthy, lovable, forgiven, or not really being free from sin. Once I allowed God to break the chains off my mind, the rest of the bondage in my life followed. I was no longer in bondage to the person that I was and all the people I had been connected to through ungodly soul ties.

Looking back over my life it seems as if I was two different people living in one body. I could smoke, drink, have sex, and do whatever else I was big and bad enough to do. On the other hand, my grades and my academics were never really an issue. I served effortlessly in church, and I was heavily involved in activities and leadership roles in organizations and community work outside of the church. It was easy for me to switch the person I needed to be from one moment to the next. This was one reason it took me so long to truly surrender and realize the amount of bondage I was in because I was still "productive and successful" in most aspects and in the eyes of most people. I had to ask God to expose me to see me for who I was.

Without the first four F's that I mentioned in the previous chapters, I would have never made it to the place where I found my own path, the one that God set out for me. Not the one based off permissive will, but the one based off His perfect will. Without faith, family/friends, forgiveness/forgetfulness, and feeding my mind I would still be lost and in bondage. I would still be continuing the cycles of generational curses that have been passed down from generation to generation. As I mentioned, I was the first to do a lot of things in my family and friends. First to get a college degree, first to get an internship, first to learn a new language, first to travel for leadership roles and conferences, first to obtain three college degrees, first to attend an HBCU and many other things. I am also the first to break the generational curses of anger, incest, sexual abuse, poverty, mentality of lack and scarcity, health issues and disease and anything else that the enemy has tried to use to destroy my family and our lineage. It stops here, and it stops with me!

My children and future generations will be generations of blessing, abundance, prosperity, freedom, and living abundantly. I refuse to go into a marriage while having sex outside of it, having to deal with infidelity and unfaithfulness of any kind, the man not being in his proper place and his role, ungodly soul ties and addictions, divorce, and any other tactic the enemy tries to use to destroy marriages and families. I am speaking against it now, rebuking it, and trusting that My God has already taken care of it all! This is the path that God has for me to be on. The path to helping others, including my family, find their path and remain on their path to freedom and living abundantly. God did not intend to send His Son to die for our freedom for us to still live in bondage to anything! That would mean that Jesus' sacrifice was for nothing. I refuse to just accept bondage or anything less than what My Savior died for me to have. To have life and have it to the full! I know that I am not perfect, nor is this world. I know things will happen that will be outside of what I would prefer to happen, but I also know that God is in control and that the things of this world are only temporary. I really have nothing to worry about or to fear. I know that my blessings will come here and when Heaven truly comes to Earth. In the meantime, I will do all that I can to make sure that His Will is done in Heaven as it is on Earth. I will not just accept or settle for less just because that is the way things are done. I will not settle for a hard life. Because I am a child of The King, I am royalty and royalty has a royal life with a royal experience. Royalty has an easy yoke and a light burden. I am in expectation for nothing less. I am believing God for the exceedingly and abundantly above all we could ask or think. I am grateful for all that I experienced and all that I went through on my journey to finding this path to freedom and living abundantly. It has equipped and prepared me to serve and share with others as they find their path to freedom and living abundantly.

"It's All in Me!"

I talked a lot all throughout this book about my past and the things that I have overcome. Some of you may be thinking, *"What is she doing now?"* Even if not, I'm about to tell you!

As I said life, success, freedom, and just about everything is a journey. At the time of writing this, I was not where I wanted to be financially, spiritually, mentally, or physically, but using the tools and strategies I have mentioned, every day I become better than I was the day before. There were days, mostly on the weekends where I ate terribly, barely drank water, didn't track what I ate, or take my nutritional supplements. *But* there have been and will continue to be more days that I do accomplish these things than not. There were days where I still had urges to masturbate, watch pornography, or have sex. There were days where I did have sex with my fiancée. I still had times where my attitude showed when it shouldn't, but God definitely isn't through with me yet! Pray for me, my mother, my therapists, and life coach who have been helping me with this. Yes, it will take a village to tame this attitude and tongue! I had days where I would stress or worry about my finances, my family or all the things that I am responsible for, but, I didn't stay there for very long. There were days where I forget to pray throughout the day or didn't focus when reading my devotions, but I kept training to get better every day. There were days where instead of sticking to the schedule I set that day, I blew most it sleeping or scrolling on Facebook, but those days were few, far and in between. There were days where I started to doubt what God is doing in and through my life with *Jalisa Ray International (Side note: The transition from branding as Jalisa Ray International instead of Empowerment Unabridged took place during the production of this publication.)*, the Young Adult Ministry, Perfect for Purpose, First Baptist Church of Guilford, Behind Closed Doors and any other opportunity that comes my way. But, every day I kept pushing forward in the vision and not focusing only on what I was seeing with my physical eye. In the midst of it all, I continued pushing forward and trained every day to be better spiritually, mentally, physically, and financially.

I made the decision as of July 30, 2017 that I will never go back to Corporate America. The success and wellbeing of *Jalisa Ray International* is my only option. It reminds me of a story about a captain and his crew headed to war.

> *In 1519, the Spanish explorer and conquistador Hernando Cortez decided that he wanted to seize the treasure that the Aztecs had been hoarding. He took 500 soldiers and 100 sailors and landed his 11 ships on the shores of the Yucatan. Despite the large army under his command, he was still vastly outnumbered by a huge and powerful empire that had been around for 600 years.*
>
> *Some of his men were unconvinced of success, and being loyal to Cuba, they tried to seize some ships to escape to there. Cortez got wind of the plot and captured the ringleaders. He wanted to make sure that the remainder of his men were completely committed to his mission and quest for riches, so he did something that seemed completely insane to his people: Cortez gave the order to scuttle his own ships.*
>
> *His men resisted, wondering how they would even get home, and his answer*

"It's All in Me!"

was: "If we are going home, we are going home in their ships!"

The path forward was clear for Cortez – All or nothing, 100% commitment. The option of failure was gone – Conquer as heroes or die.

The ships were sunk – He kept a single ship to send back the "royal fifth" (the king of Spain claimed 20% of all treasures). By doing this, the level of commitment of the men was raised to an extreme level, much higher than anyone could have imagined.

Incredibly, they succeeded in this unlikely feat. In six hundred years, no one else had been able to conquer the Aztecs and plunder their riches. They were able to do it simply because there was no choice, no fallback – the ships were gone, the only alternative was death.

I have made the decision to do whatever it takes to build and succeed with being a business owner and building *Jalisa Ray International* to a multi-billion-dollar company. Some may call this greedy or lofty, but I have a large and long legacy that I am leaving. None of the future generations in my bloodline will experience poverty or scarcity on my accord. If they choose that life on their own that will be a different story. They will know that they are royalty and the bloodline that they come from is wealthy and prosperous. Not on just this Earth, but in Heaven. They will know that their family is a family of strong faith and belief in God, that their ancestors fought for them to not have to struggle like we did. Some people told me not to burn bridges and when it comes to the jobs I had, and I did not. In my mind though, I have. There is no going back. I have decided, cut off every other option, to build this legacy for future generations to stand and build on. This book and the others that I will write will be a part of this legacy that I am building upon. They will know what it took to get to where they are and how to stay there from these books.

From past generations some things will stick and stay, but for other things they have had to be uprooted for a better future for our legacy and bloodline. The generational curses are no more, and the generational blessings are continuing to outpour. The legacy will not only impact my family and bloodline, but the entire world. God called us to take His Word to all the ends of the Earth and that is what my family and I will do until Jesus comes again! For me, there are no other options mainly because I have surrendered to what God is calling me to do. I refuse to continue to be disobedient to His plan for my life. As you can see I walked contrary to His plan for my life for many years. Taking the vision He gave me back in 2013, and now actually running with it is making the difference in my life and the lives of those that I speak, preach, teach, and coach through *Jalisa Ray International*. This is truly only the beginning. Here is a list of goals I have set for my life:

- I am looking forward to reaching my goals of losing 40 lbs.
- Replenishing my initial emergency fund to $3,000
- Getting married to my future husband Anthony J. Hardy and having all his children
- Completing my M. Div. and my PhD in Natural Medicine
- Becoming a Reverend
- Completing additional certifications related to health and finance
- Continuing to gain wisdom and knowledge from my current and future coaches and mentors

"IT'S ALL IN ME!"

- Staying abstinent until getting married in 2018
- Making *Jalisa Ray International* a global organization
- Finishing this book and publishing it by February of 2018
- Retiring my parents within the next two years
- Watching my boys finish college and then go off to the NFL
- Building a big house for my family and I to live in
- Seeing my brother-in-law saved
- Seeing my sister free from all the things in her past
- Seeing my family free of physical dis-eases
- Writing and publishing more books
- Being able to give back and pay it forward all the things and people that poured into me

Where I am today is a sample picture of where I will be in one year, five years, 10 years and beyond. I am truly excited about my future and the way that I got here in spite of all of the things that I have had to go through. I appreciate all the good and the bad that have occurred in my life because they all contributed to who I am today and where I am going tomorrow. For me, and for you, finding our own path will mean getting in step and staying in step with God, continuously surrendering our lives to Him, taking one step at a time and not worrying about what the next will look like, and embracing and enjoying each moment. I must always remind myself and the people that I encounter that life is a journey.

    We have the expectations that by a certain age, we should have it all together. We compare ourselves to what we see other people doing in their lives, most times on social media, and we get discouraged about where we are in life. Yes, we are all capable of doing more than we do or have done, but we cannot dwell on what we haven't done or what someone else has done that we've wanted to do. We must focus on what we can do in the moment to further our individual journey. We cannot walk in the shoes of anyone else, but we can walk in the footsteps of Christ. No one is ever an overnight success, you just don't know what they went through to get to where they are. You won't be an overnight success either. It will be a lifetime journey to truly get to the place where you have given your all and done all you can. The work will not stop even once we get to Heaven. He's not just preparing us for the work here, but He is preparing us for eternity. This life is only temporary, so we cannot get caught up on it. Being caught up on the temporary takes our focus off what is eternal.

The morning of September 11 at two-thirty, I received a call from my sister waking me up out of my sleep. I had made a conscious decision to go to sleep at a decent time so by 11pm I was knocked out! I woke up to her saying that AJ has been trying to get in contact with me, he told her there was a fire and that he'd lost everything. Still half-asleep and in a daze, I called him back to see what was going on. He is the type of guy to not let much of anything get to him. He was very calm for the most part about losing everything. I could tell he was a bit frazzled when I first talked to him, but as the day progressed he was actually laughing and making jokes about it. He said to me, "Life is too short and too long to take everything so seriously. I am alive, and no one got hurt. I will be fine." This really made me fall in love with him all over again. I cannot say that I would be the same way if I was in the same situation. It made me think of how much emphasis I put on material things. On the things that are only temporary. We stress ourselves out over jobs, money, accomplishments, cars, houses, and bills. These things we cannot take with us to Heaven nor will they matter to us when we are much older. We have to have a forever perspective with a right now focus. The things right now will not last forever, but there are things we need to do with what we have right now before we get to forever.

This book seemed to turn into journal entries. As I was writing I would include what was going on in my life at the time. It turned into a play by play of where my life was at the time of writing this book. I will eventually turn it into a journal for others to obtain healing from going through my journey and theirs at the same time. I realized that I was in a place where I was being tested to continue to share my testimony. That the mess that my life consisted of was for the message I have to share with the world. The events that took place during the time I was writing this book showed me that. Not only did my future husband lose everything, my family had an emergency which called for me to use $1,100 of my emergency fund to help. I had been living off my emergency fund since probably May or June of 2017, after the money I had was spent on bills, my business, and other family stuff. So, for me, this was devastating. I contemplated being selfish and not helping, but that was out of fear. At the time I did not know where my next dollar would come from. This sacrifice was more than I could prepare myself for. I am grateful that I had the money to help, but it brought up a lot of fear and anxiety which I did not know was there. I started to cry when I finally decided to say I would help. I felt guilty because now I was not being a cheerful giver, but I did it anyway. Not only because the emergency affected me, but because that's what I do for my family, I give, and I make sacrifices. Being down to my last at that point, right after deciding to stick with building *Jalisa Ray International* and not going back to Corporate America, was a big blow! It made me second guess my decision for a moment, but then I started to think about my reaction to the situation. I started to ask God what lesson He wanted me to learn from the situation. Because of my faith and obedience God made a way for my mother to pay me back not even a week later.

    My faith was being tested. God wants me to trust Him and Him alone. If I had that money in the bank that I relied on and felt like it was my protection I was not relying completely on God. That situation helped me come to a place where I had no choice, but to rely totally on Him. Financially, I had been in the place where I had struggled the most with trusting God. Having to deplete my savings to help my family showed me just how much my faith lacked in that area. I started to blame others, point fingers, and get angry, but I know that God allows and/or does everything for a reason. The reason is so that He can get the glory and for our good. This literally has come full circle back to faith. Our path ends and begins with faith. I started this book with the first F being faith and as my story unfolded it came back to faith.

I said something at a financial workshop at Coppin State I did around the time of writing this book. I said that my feelings around money are in between faith and fear, which should not have been the case and really cannot be the case. But that is where I was wavering in my faith. The two, faith and fear, cannot coexist. It is either one or the other. I realized that I had not been walking in faith as much as I thought when it came to my finances. I allowed it to hold me back in my business. I would use it as an excuse. I would say, "I am not where I want to be financially so there is no way I could help someone else with their finances." I was reminded by more than one person in my village that my gift and calling had more to it than how much money I did or did not have in my accounts. I was reminded that there are people who, even though I am not where I want to be, to them, I am still seen as an expert. I was reminded that my circumstances do not negate my calling. I was reminded that wealth is about way more than just money. It starts with your mindset. God has truly renewed my mindset when it comes to wealth. The wisdom and knowledge God has blessed me with is what I want to share with others, so they can be financially free and live abundantly.

As I said, if I had that money in the bank I was walking in what I thought was faith. It was not faith because my sense of security came from the money I was able to see in my accounts. Having to just about empty out two of my accounts showed me otherwise. I was walking in a false faith which is ultimately fear. It was not based on what I did not see, but what I could see. I realized just how much I was idolizing money and allowing it to keep me in bondage. This situation was a true eye opener. I realized that I am still blessed beyond belief and I have

"It's All in Me!"

everything that I need. God had to show me that even if I have nothing else He is all I need, and He has everything that I need.

In the midst of the situation I could not see this through the immediate feelings of fear, frustration, anxiety, and doubt. Afterwards I was able to see through a lens of hope and peace. For the most part. I automatically went into "fix it" mode instead of turning it over to God to fix it. I automatically started to think about ideas for how to make some money with my businesses. I started to think about people I could call. I even thought about putting up a GoFundMe page. I had to sit back and say, "Okay, God. You have it all under control. You've already worked it out for my good and Your glory." He has given me tasks to do, one being writing this book. I couldn't allow one situation to cause me to lose focus or get off track with the things that He had already given me to do. I was trying to figure out other things to do when He has already showed me what to do. I continue to take things one day at a time. I continued to work on finishing this book, doing the speaking engagements I had lined up, and preparing for other upcoming events and programs.

I had to really do what my business coach had been telling me and enjoy the journey and do what the Word says to count it all joy. I decided that I would switch things up one day. After going to babysit where I ended up being late to get the child off of the bus, I decided that I would go to the library instead of going home. I needed to change my scenery and the energy around me. I was reminded also in the midst of the family/financial situation that in order to get different results I had to do something different. So, I stepped outside of my comfort zone and went to the library to write and get other things done. I talked to my business coach about everything and I told her how I felt like just giving up. I felt like the more steps I took forward, the more I got knocked back. She reminded me that giving up is exactly what the enemy wants me to do. I was reminded that there are current and future generations waiting for me to come and speak to them, coach them, and to read this book.

She told me I couldn't give up or give in to my current and temporary circumstances. That is where I was during the writing of this book on my journey to freedom and living abundantly.

I always must remind myself of the things that I tell my audiences and my clients that this life is a journey, not a destination. I am learning to be content in every situation and circumstance, so that no matter what comes my way I will not quit. When God was showing up and showing out I was okay, but as soon as things that were outside of my control began to happen I would unravel. I would begin to doubt the plan that I was so sure about. I would begin to rethink the decisions that I had made.

This is exactly what the enemy wanted. If I give up and start to doubt, then that means he wins. Why would I allow a loser and someone who has already been defeated to win? That would be ridiculous. That is what fear is, having the faith that the enemy will prevail with the situation or circumstance at hand. Christ's sacrifice already made a way for us to have victory and dominion over everything. That family/financial situation looked like a giant or my own personal Goliath, but God is bigger. He had already worked it out. I do not have to fear or worry about how my financial situation will get taken care of. I do not have to worry about where my next check will come from. I know that God has called me to greater and that He will provide for me. It may not seem like it now, but I have enough faith and expectation to receive the vision and the provision that He has shown me.

I had no clue how it was going to work out and I am learning to be okay with that. Let me repeat, I am learning to be okay with that, this is part of my journey. In this journey of life if you are not learning, you are not growing. So, as I learned from this situation and allowed God to build my faith, I embraced where I was because it was only temporary. When you can embrace where you are and where you come from, it makes where you're going so much sweeter and much more appreciated. This is a part of my path and I am grateful for it.

"It's All in Me!"

Being this transparent and open with my life will not be for everyone nor will everyone agree, but there is someone out there that needs to hear this part of my story in detail. Not just the parts that will come in my future, but where I am today. People will see the success, but a lot of successful people don't talk about the struggle until after they have reached success. My journey to freedom and living abundantly calls for me to share my journey with the world along the way. It will not be easy or comfortable, but that does not matter to me as much as the people that I will help by doing so.

The day the family/financial situation happened I almost did not write for this book. I almost allowed the situation, which is now a thing of the past, to dictate my future and control my feelings. I stayed in bed until almost three-thirty. I had not eaten anything except a blueberry muffin nor had I done anything other than get up to use the bathroom and scroll through social media. I had to push through the way I was feeling and decide to feel differently. I almost went home after leaving from babysitting. I went to one library and it was closing at seven, so I decided to drive to the other one that closed at nine instead. Sometimes, we must push past how we feel and push past the roadblocks to get to where we need to go and to do the things that we need to do.

I almost got discouraged when I heard someone talking about things that are like the message that I have for *Jalisa Ray International*. Instead, I shared the message and reminded myself that just because the message is the same, the messenger is different. The people that will hear their message will hear it and the people that will hear my message will hear it. It is not about competition, but about the impact that we make for the Kingdom. It is not about me or them, but it is about Him. God made us all unique so there is no such thing as competition when it comes to our purpose. So, as I continue to find my own path which is walking in faith instead of sight, I am allowing God to lead my steps. I am constantly reminded that it is not about me at all. It is about all the people that will be impacted by what God is using me to do. I am simply a vessel, a messenger for God to build up His Kingdom. Instead of me focusing on my situation, I must make a conscious decision to stay focused on God. The path or next step may not always be clear but that's when you know you're walking in faith on your own path.

When you don't know what the next step is or where the path may lead, keep stepping even when it is dark, knowing that God's got you. Knowing that He will take care of you and knowing that no matter what steps you take that God will work it all out for your good and His glory. God is making sure that in my situation, only He will get the glory. He knows His child and He knows that I can be big headed, so He is humbling me. He is making sure that when people hear my story they know that it was Him that made it all possible and not me. As you and I can see, I am human, and I am weak, but in Him and with Him, I am strong. In Him, I can do the impossible. Without Him, I am nothing. This chapter is the last of the F's. So, I am going to do a recap of all five and bring a close to this chapter in my life's story. The next chapter will reflect this journey of writing this book and what you can look to expect next from me and *Jalisa Ray International*.

For the recap I am going to reiterate the 5 F's and the sub-points I gave for each. I will not give subpoints for the last F because that is all up to you. You must decide which, if any, of the Five F's, you're going to use on your journey to freedom and living abundantly. You must decide whether you're going to go along with God's perfect will or settle for His permissive will. You're going to have to decide for yourself whether you're going to follow God or the enemy/world. I have shared my story, the things I went through, and what helped me to get through them. This book is not just for you, but it was for me too. It is part of my journey to freedom, healing, wholeness, and living abundantly. Writing and publishing this was a journey in and of itself. With all the people that mentioned to me to write a book, all of the book titles God had given me, and knowing my testimony would help others, it was only a matter of time before I got it done. I completed the writing ahead of schedule!

"It's All in Me!"

As you can see God worked out the editing, cover creation, publishing, printing, and all the other little details that went along with the publishing of this book. It was not all a piece of cake it stretched me in so many ways, but for you to be reading it right now, it was all worth it.

The Five F's and their sub-points are as follows:

1. **Faith**
   a. Evaluate where you are in your relationship with God
   b. Look back over your life and see where God has brought you from
   c. Acknowledge it and ask God to help you to let it go and take responsibility for how you will respond to it and use it from now on
   d. Look for ways that will help you to strengthen your relationship and faith in God: Read His Word, seek spiritual guidance/mentorship, look for a fellowship of believers to join and get involved with, seek out people that you can help to mentor or give back to, when you have a decision to make seek His guidance and move in faith even in the face of fear.
   e. Truly and totally surrender your life to Him: This does not require you to do anything but to just *be with Him* and allow Him to move and do things in your life and through you
2. **Family/Friends**
   a. Evaluate where I am in my relationship with God
   b. Evaluate the people that you spend most of your time with
   c. Evaluate the level of reciprocity in your relationships and your motives behind what you bring to the relationship
3. **Forgiveness/Forgetfulness (I didn't give these earlier, did you notice?)**
   a. Don't let anyone tell you how to forgive. It's a journey and a process all in one
   b. Don't wait too long to forgive, when we wait to forgive we hinder our own blessing including our forgiveness and blocking our prayers (Mark 11:25)
   c. Understand that because of Jesus's sacrifice God forgave you for all of your sins, who are you not to forgive someone else,

and for that matter even to not forgive yourself. His forgiveness trumps all forgiveness!
   d. There will be certain situations where it will be necessary to forgive God even though for some we might not acknowledge or realize it, don't be afraid to let God know exactly how you feel.
   e. Take the journey to forgiveness which does include forgetfulness, contrary to popular belief, one day, one step, and one moment at a time.
   f. BONUS: Just because you have forgiven them and have done your best to forget what they have done or didn't do, it does not require reconciliation. Use *Godly* wisdom and guidance to decide whether to reconcile in the midst of or afterwards

4. **Feed Your Mind**
   a. Evaluate and make note of what you tell yourself daily for at least one week.
   b. Evaluate and make note of what forms of media you take in and how much time you spend doing so daily for at least a week
   c. Plan time into your day to read, study, and meditate on the Word to make it a habit and part of your daily routine. Start out with 10-15 minutes if you feel as if you don't have enough time to do so or get up earlier.
   d. Research and identify books and other positive materials to partake in daily for at least 10-15 minutes to make it a part of your daily routine.
   e. Research and contact a mentor, therapist, life coach, or someone you can talk to about the negative thoughts you have and the addictions you may have identified when it comes to mainstream media, social media, or anything else you may have discovered during your time of self-evaluation.

5. **Find Your Own Path**

Reflection Questions:

1. Looking back at your life, what were some decisions you've made that were not truly on the Path that God laid out for you?

　
　
　
　

2. Which of the Five F's has impact your journey to freedom and living abundantly? Why?

　
　
　
　

3. Which of the Five F's do you feel you need to improve in the most? Why?

4. How has this book impacted your journey to freedom and living abundantly?

_____
_____
_____
_____

My prayer for you:

Heavenly Father,

You are truly worthy to be praised! Thank You again for the person reading the book. Thank You for the journey that they have been on and will continue even after they finish reading this part of my journey. Thank You that they had the heart to continue to make it this far in the book. Some things in their life may have been triggered or dug up, so I ask that You provide them with the resources to deal with and heal from these things. Father God, I thank You for the path that you have set out just for this person. For the tests that will be testimonies, for the mess that will be a message, and for all the things in their life and their story that You will use to help someone else. Give them the desire to share their story so that they can heal and that they can be a light and a help to someone else that may be going through something similar. Even if they are in the midst of it give them the strength to share it for their healing and for someone else's. Thank You for continuing to cover and protect them. Thank You for working everything in their life out for their good and Your glory. When they are done reading this book continuously remind them of these five F's and any other tools and strategies they can use on their journey to freedom and living abundantly. God thank You so much for their freedom from the things of this world, from generational curses, from financial bondage, from health bondage, from relationship bondage, and any other bondage that they may be experiencing. Thank You for defeating the enemy and constantly reminding them that even though the devil has and will try that he is already defeated and that he cannot win in their lives. Thank You God for their life, health, and strength. God give them all that they need to continue this life's journey. Give them the desire to fulfill all their purpose and calling so that when You return Jesus that they will have done all that they could do for You. If they are not saved, they do not know you, or may not have wanted to know You, stir it up in their hearts even now to want that relationship with You, to want to know You, and to want to be saved right now in the name of Jesus. Let them be ready and prepared for when You return! Thank You again for them taking this time to read my story and I pray that they share it with someone else that may need it. You are an awesome God and even that is not a big enough word to describe You! Let them praise You in Spirit and in truth and let Your perfect will be done in their lives! Thank You in advance for hearing and answering this prayer! I am believing You for this and much more God!

In Jesus' name I pray,

Amen!

Chapter 6: Reflections

Writing this book was literally a lifelong journey. From the very beginning even before the world began God set in place for this book to be written and read by you. It was predestined for me to experience all of the things that I have experienced, since the writing and publishing of this book. That is also the publishing date for this book. It was not by happenstance that I went through these things and that you picked up this book having gone through or will be going through some of the same things. This is the first of many books. Not just my book, but your book as well. You have a story to tell just like I do. There are people out there that need to hear your story. If only one person reads this book and is inspired to tell their story and write their story, then it served its purpose. My desire is that this book will inspire people to open up and tell someone their story whether in a book, video, social media post, to one other person, in a group of people or any other way you can think of. Telling our story is a part of our healing journey and a part of the healing journey of someone else. We all have or will go through things that may take the wind out of our sails but knowing that someone may have gone through something similar, the same, or maybe even worse and they didn't give up makes a world of a difference. I have not made it to where I want to be as I said before, but I am on a journey to be better and think better every day.

Publishing this book would not have been possible without God, my business coach, and the encouragement of my amazing support village. It took a village for me to get to this point. Again, to all of you I say, thank you. If I had to go back and write all the names of everyone this book would be thousands of pages long with names and stories of how they contributed to my story and the publishing of this book. I am amazed that it took me less than a month to write this book. The freedom to sit down and pour my heart out was so healing! I was not worried about what it would sound like or go back to see if it made sense. I barely experienced writer's block at all going through the first phase of writing. There were brief moments where I would have to pause and regroup but that was it, just moments. I would sit down and each time during the hour a day I would manage to write between 1,500 to almost 3,000 words during each session. I had the thought some days to write for more than an hour, but I did not want to rush the process. The things that I shared from day-to-day made this journey special and beneficial on my journey to freedom and living abundantly.

I realized through this writing, editing, and publishing process just how much writing is a gift that God has given me to use for His glory and the uplifting of His Kingdom. Every day I sat down to write I felt excited and energized. Even on those days where I had a rough day and didn't really feel like writing, once I started it was a breeze. I can recall one day that was a really rough day. I just barely made it to 1500 words which was the original goal I had set to write daily. It was about nine in the evening and I was tired from the day. But I had to get over my feelings and write anyway. I consistently wrote every single weekday for at least an hour or at least 1500 words for 20 weekdays. From August 17, 2017-September 13, 2017. This is a testament in and of itself of the self-discipline and the consistency that I used to eliminate the doubt that I had. It took me setting a date and setting a time every day to write. Even though some days it wasn't exactly at 1pm, I still made it a priority to write. I have gone back, read over this, and have been blown away because I know that it was God writing through me. He gave me the self-discipline and the consistency. He gave me the time-freedom to do it. It is all because of Him. He made this possible. He made this dream become a reality for such a time as this.

I know as I have said many times before that this book was not just for you, but it was for me too. To be able to write 20+ years' worth of my story and experiences in 20 days was an amazing experience. It helped me to better understand myself, the people in my life, God, and

"It's All in Me!"

what God has done and will do in my life. This is one reason I would say for everyone to write and share their life story because as you share it is learning experience for everyone involved.

This is something that I plan to continue to do every 5-10 years or so in my life's journey. To share with you and with future generations of my family. I plan to write along with my future husband, a book about our journey together and getting to the altar. That one is going to be crazy! To see our story from both points of view.

I was given the idea one morning after talking with my business coach and praying about another chapter for the book. To write my story in a condensed version in chronological order. In the other chapters my story is in bits and pieces. I will try not to be redundant, but certain parts are important and worth repeating. Let's move on to chapter 7, the Abridged version of my life story.

Chapter 7: The Abridged Version of my Journey to Freedom and Living Abundantly

In this chapter, I will be sharing the condensed version of my whole life story from start to finish. This was not even a thought until I was almost done writing the other six chapters of this book. I realized that my story in the previous chapters is in bits and pieces. So, to give you a complete picture and maybe clear some things up, I am going to give you the whole story. So, sit back, relax, and enjoy!

My mom was born in Buffalo, NY and my dad was born in Lackawanna, NY which was not far from each other. Both were married before, but never had any children by their previous spouses. My dad, who's middle name means womanizer, did just that. My dad worked with my aunt, my mom's sister, at a part time job. My aunt introduced my mom to my dad after talking him up to her about him. At first my mom was not really interested, but since my aunt was persistent she gave him a chance. They talked over the phone for a while and once they met, my dad came to my mom's house and never left. My mom being a Pastor's daughter, born and raised in the church, knew that she couldn't keep living in sin with my dad, so she told him that either they would have to get married or he would have to leave. So, they got married because even before things got serious and when she tried to get rid of him he wouldn't let her. The first three years into the marriage things were fine. After thinking that neither of them could have kids my sister was conceived. My mom had two miscarriages before my sister. Things began to get rocky as my dad went back to his womanizing ways. He decided that he wanted to have his cake and eat it too. My mom put him out because it had become too much stress and drama. They were still married so they still did what married people did. My mom refused to disobey God by sleeping with someone that wasn't her husband. Because of this I was conceived about two and a half years into their separation. Ironically, I was conceived at a family function in Maryland where we later relocated to. For almost five years, she was technically a single mother. My dad was around just about every day still, but it wasn't the same for me, at least. My sister had those two years to bond with him and she is the true definition of a Daddy's girl.

I, on the other hand, was all about our mommy. Being sickly and her having to stay home with me for three years until I could go off to school full-time, I spent most of my time with her. Yes, I do still call her mommy and I call my father daddy. The entire time my father played around, my mom stayed faithful, by the grace of God and her obedience to Him. Had it not been for God telling her to wait for Him to work things out she would have been out playing too. My conception was a blessing and a bit of a curse because of the brokenness of my parent's relationship. While pregnant with me, my mom dealt with a lot of stress and had a lot of anger and frustration she was dealing with daily because of my dad. This translated into me being a cry baby, an angry child, teenager, and young adult. The feelings she had I experienced as well while she was carrying me. They said that I was born with an angry face even, that I looked like a bulldog.

I was not too fond of my father for a majority of my childhood and adolescent life. When he came around I wasn't too interested unless he was feeding me or bought me something. If he stayed around too long I would ask when he was going home. Those daddy issues started early. I had my grandfather who was probably closer to a father figure than my dad growing up. He was "Big Bucket" and I was "Little Bucket" because of our big heads. He took me everywhere, fed me, and carried me around. I was attached to him like my sister was attached to my father. His favorite ice cream is vanilla and growing up so was mine. He is still my heart. He has Alzheimer's now and barely remembers me. Now that we live in Maryland, I rarely get to see him. The last time I saw him there were glimpses of times where I knew he remembered me. I've been holding onto those moments as the disease continues to take over.

"It's All in Me!"

I was a very advanced child. I learned to walk, talk, read, and be potty trained early. My mom said I sounded like Minnie Mouse because I didn't give my voice the chance to develop. She also thought I would be a midget because in my pre-k class when all the kids sat in their chairs their feet touched the floor, mine did not. This is what happens when you have an older sibling you follow around. Unfortunately, in my case it was both beneficial and detrimental. I began to explore boys and boyfriends in pre-k as I mentioned before my first boyfriend was Eric. My mom said I would ask from an early age for a long time when I could have a boyfriend. She finally told me 30, so that I would stop asking. I was the teacher's pet because I was advanced and to keep me occupied I helped my classmates with their work. This was my life when it came to school, the advanced, GT, honor roll scholar type of child. I excelled in anything that was put in front of me.

On the other hand, I was exposed to a whole other world that unfortunately, I excelled in as well. The world of masturbation, pornography, incest, and sexual abuse. It seems to me looking back that I always had this double-life scenario going on. In some cases, triple because I was one way at home, one way at school, and another way at church. I was so messed up and confused. The enemy from the very beginning did everything he could to destroy me. I realized later that him trying to make sure that my windpipe and esophagus were fused shut was for him to keep me quiet for me not to be able to tell my story. The enemy knew that God called me because my mom gave us back to God as soon as we were born. I was dedicated to Him in her womb that night she went to the church and had them pray over me. So, the enemy knew that there was some damage to be done to his kingdom through me. He even went so far as to use the person who was literally my "second mother" growing up, to try to destroy me. He tried to use the generational curses in my bloodline to destroy me. The drug abuse and alcohol addictions, the promiscuity, the anger, the fighting, and so much more he tried to use them all to destroy me.

As I said I do not recall everything just parts of things that I have discussed with family and friends. And the sexual abuse I only remember parts of. In the other world that I excelled in, I brought others with me. I did sexual things with male cousins while we played "house" growing up. I am not sure when the stuff that was happening with my sister stopped either. I think it was between ages 10-13 when we moved from Buffalo, NY to Maryland. I did all elementary school there and part of middle school. When we moved to Maryland, they wanted to put me in 8th grade instead of 6th. My mom said no because she didn't want me around all of those older kids and grow up too fast. She had no clue that it was already too late. At the age of 13, as I said, is when I started to officially have sex and wasn't engaging in incest. I hate to use the word incest because it brings so much guilt. As a child, I did not know any better, but incest is what it was. Side note, if this is like your situation and your story, do not allow the enemy to keep you in bondage to the guilt of it. I have had difficulties with attaching the words incest and sexual abuse to the things that I went through and did it because in all actuality the situations that occurred were not our fault. I had to even look up the definitions of the words incest and sexual abuse to be sure. By definition, that is what occurred, but my sister and I were doing what was done to us. We had no clue it was wrong as young children.

In middle school, I was bullied and talked about because I was very different from everyone else. I talked and dressed differently, I was what was considered fat to other middle schoolers, I wore nerdy glasses, and I was still a year ahead of where I was supposed to be, so I was considered a nerd. Looking back at old school pictures I probably would have picked on me too if I were them. I started to sort of come into my own after graduating and going to high school. I think I was in with the "cool kids," but I really had a diverse group of friends and was

"IT'S ALL IN ME!"

cool with a lot of people because of my diverse personality. I was active and involved, intellectual, and just seemed to get along with everyone for the most part. I got into one fight my entire life that I can remember and that was my 8th grade year. After that in high school I almost got into a fight because this girl leaked some pictures I had sent to a guy I was talking to at the time to the whole school. I told my mom and she called the office who snatched me up before I could get to the girl. I learned my lesson. I stopped sending pictures after that, of course right?

I had a very cultured experience in high school to say the least. I was involved in my academics with honors classes, I was involved in extracurricular activities such as Spanish club, leadership-business club, and I ran track my senior year. I probably did other things, but I don't recall. I had a core group of female and male friends that were close knit. After we graduated, we all went our separate ways for the most part. I went off to a college where no one from my high school nor middle school attended. Throughout high school I stayed on top of academics, but I still managed to manipulate people, so that I could leave class when I wanted to. I became close with the security guards and they would not bother me about roaming the halls or leaving the school when I wanted to go smoke or go be with one of the guys I was dealing with that didn't go to my school. In high school my mom had to threaten to put me away because I kept going missing. I would leave school with friends or guys and come home when I felt like it.

One of the times I went missing I was raped by two guys who were friends of a guy I was dating at the time. They told me that he couldn't take me home because his mom was coming home. They said the only way that I would get home was to let them have their way with me. Being 13 and not having a phone and not knowing where I was I just let it happen. The guy that I was dealing with at the time didn't help at all. He came back around when they were done and then took me home. It took me years to understand or come to the terms that it was rape. For years I blamed myself because I put myself in that predicament. I had so much guilt and shame behind it that I allowed it to cause me to continue to give myself a way to men. I felt as if I had given myself to the men that raped me. Years later, I reached out to the guy I was dealing with on my journey to forgiveness. He apologized for it and told me he has a daughter now that he would not want anything like that to happen to. Sometimes you'll get an apology and sometimes you won't, but that shouldn't stop you from forgiving. Just because it was not a forceful rape does not mean it was not rape. If you did not want it, it was rape even if you did not fight it. Do not allow people to blame you for what someone else did to you.

My life has been a real roller coaster with lots of hill, valley's, twists and turns. I spent a lot of time upside down and on my back. It was nothing but God that got me out of those situations that could have gone another way.

After high school, I really started to feel myself. I got my first job after graduating and I started to really figure out what I thought I wanted to do with my life. I had planned to go to Spain for a year to study abroad. I started to raise money for it on gofundme.com but did not get much at all. One day my Auntie Joyce told me she was taking me on a college tour to Coppin State University in Baltimore. I had never really been in Baltimore to see what it was about before then. I just knew it was what some considered to be "the hood." Which is where I came from, so I really didn't want to go back. Once I got to the school though I really liked it. At the time it was a smaller more intimate campus. It had a family feel to it. I ended up going on my tour and getting accepted the same day into the honors program based off my age, grades, and SAT scores. My tuition and books were taken care of. It was not what I wanted to do, but God ordered my footsteps the entire time for me to get to where I am today. In College is where I did more experimenting and "finding myself."

I had a freedom that I did not have before. I did everything that I thought I was big and bad enough to do. I had health issues and,

"It's All in Me!"

eventually, was kicked out of the honors program. I also did a lot of amazing things and met a lot of amazing people. I founded a short-lived chapter of The National Society of Leadership and Success at Coppin, I was an RA where I impacted many college students with daily interaction and programs, I worked with the First Year Experience program, I co-founded a health and science major initiative organization, I joined Alpha Nu Omega Sorority, Inc. where I held leadership positions each year I was on campus, and so much more. I got a full college experience and there is where I met the love of my life, my future husband, my best friend, Anthony J. Hardy.

Even though I didn't continue to pursue the career that initially set out to pursue as a Pharmacist the experience that I received, the relationships that I have built and lost, and the way that it matured me, I would not change it for the world. I decided my senior year that I no longer wanted to be a Pharmacist because I realized I was only doing it for the money. I would not be happy supporting and promoting the same health system that failed me time after time. I did some research that year and found Dr. Stephanie Reid who was close to the school at the time. Prior to that what contributed to my decision was being introduced to the health and wellness industry through a company named Zija International. It was my first experience with Network Marketing that changed my life, my perspective on health, my career choice, and my goals.

I saw how natural supplements changed people's lives including mine. Once I found Dr. Reid and connected with her. She agreed to mentor me and allowed me to come work with her at her practice after I graduated. The rest is history. I still finished out my time at Coppin to get the degrees in Biology and General Chemistry because I had already accumulated the debt for them and I like to finish what I start. I still tried to use the degrees after graduating. I had played in different Network marketing opportunities, but never really took them seriously because I didn't want to do that hard work. I would sit, learn, go to seminars, and talk to coaches and mentors. I would do the learning and take some action here and there, but it was not consistent at all. I did learn so much that contributes to the building of my businesses today and I still have a mentor from when I started in MLM back in 2011, Brian Beane. I had a job as an optician which I loved, but the environment wasn't conducive for my growth and where God was taking me. Had I stayed there I would have gone into another direction I was not meant to go in. After that job I did not get another job for almost a year. I continued to work with Dr. Reid.

Then, in 2015, I was asked to assist Minister Breanne Stewart, a member of my church at the time that I didn't really know, to help build her ministry. I agreed, and I helped her as her Executive Assistant and VP for almost two years. I landed in the childcare field by happenstance. My godmother, Robin Powell, in Orlando, FL, called me one day randomly asking me if I had gotten a job. I told her no and she proceeded to tell me about a friend who was a big director of a child care center. I babysat all the time for family, so I knew how to take care of children. It was something I loved to do, but never thought about working at a center until then. I contacted my godmother's friend who helped me get the job. I ended up getting hired about a week after she got fired. I got there, and I got comfortable. I had some issues as most do in the childcare field, but I loved the kids that I had in my class as if they were my own. I was thinking about moving up in the company, but I always knew in the back of my mind that I wanted to own my own business. I knew that I did not want to work for someone else the rest of my life. I knew that I wanted to get my doctorate degree in Natural Medicine so that I could eventually open my own practice and/or practice alongside Dr. Reid.

I still stayed there making plans to move up in the company, making plans to use the money I was making there to continue to pay off my debt. Then one random day in January of this year, I got a call from a friend who used to work for the center I was currently working for. She wanted me to come over to the company she was working for as Assistant Director in training for almost $4 more than I was making at the company I was currently working for. It was a tough decision, but the immediate promotion and the extra money caught my attention. I went back and forth about the decision, but I finally decided to go. It was one of the hardest decisions I ever had to make. I later realized it was also one of the worst and best decisions I had ever made as well. I decided that after all the drama and madness that I experienced there I would quit after only working there two months. I told them that it was for the purposes of me finishing school and my minister in training process. I started another Bachelor of Science Degree in Natural Health in September of 2014. I also started my minister in training process at the end of 2015 after much pushing, prodding, and being pulled up by God and other people about it. That was not a part of my plan, but it was all in God's plan. God moving me from one center to the next was His way of getting me outside of my comfort zone to get to where He wanted me to be. The place I am now as a full-time entrepreneur trusting Him for the vision and surrendering to His path for my life. I had to take the long route because I'm hard headed and apparently really from Missouri, the show me state. I would not have been here, and I would not be writing my book because I would have stayed comfortable at the first childcare center. I would have taken an even longer and much harder route to get here. So I am grateful for the experience that I had at the last center which is what made it the best and worst decision I had ever made job wise anyway.

    Even after quitting my job and deciding I would focus on my relationship with God, finishing school, and my minister in training process I was still in a place where I felt unfulfilled and weighed down. I was still applying for other jobs and looking into other opportunities to make some money because of course as time went on my main bank accounts started to dwindle and I had to live off my Emergency Fund which I was hoping that I would not have to do. I set goals for what I wanted to do financially, but in the back of my mind once things got rough, I went back to applying for jobs and trying to figure things out on my own. I mentioned the day I was led to share my testimony on Facebook and the interview I was asked to do on a friend of mine's show.

Even after that getting confirmation and saying that I was a full-time entrepreneur, I still had other options I was looking into and thinking about. This was because I still had fear and doubt sitting on my shoulders telling me that the vision God gave me was impossible. That I had given up on this vision and other things God has brought to me when it comes to business. That I would not stick with it this time because I did not any other time before since 2011 when I officially started my journey to entrepreneurship. *Jalisa Ray International* at the time in my mind was still just one of those things I was trying to do, but not actually making the moves to do. In July is when I decided that I would join my business coaches official coaching program called Women Who Finish. I was tired of starting things and not finishing them. I was tired of starting with *Jalisa Ray International* and quitting on it. I was tired of not being consistent with achieving my goals. Taking that step to get the help that I needed and the accountability that this coaching program provides has been the continuous push I needed. Going through the coaching program and working with Robyn-Ann had built up my passion and my confidence in myself and what God has gifted me to do. He has given me everything and everyone that I need in order to succeed in carrying out the vision God has given me for *Jalisa Ray International*. In November of 2017 Robyn-Ann disbanded the program but God still provided. She has been there for me checking in with me and coaching me every step of the way. Towards the end of Women Who Finish a sorority sister of mine from the business and professional sorority started Mad Money University. MMU is a group coaching membership that has been a true blessing to

"It's All in Me!"

me on my journey to building *Jalisa Ray International* and publishing this book.

For me, I do not ever recall there being specific turning points in my life. There have always been a series of things that occurred for me to get to a certain place in my life. It has been the same thing for me in my journey of building *Jalisa Ray International*. It has been the same thing with my bondage to sin and soul-ties. It has been the same thing in my journey to holistic health. And probably every other journey that makes up the journey that is my life. These things all consisted of a series of decisions that I made from obedience and sometimes sacrifice that led up to something else. My life has been a puzzle but not just any old puzzle, one of those puzzles that looking at the pieces or even looking at what seems like the whole picture, it rarely makes sense. I am learning to get used to not understanding everything or everything not making sense. It has made my life so much more fun and interesting even though sometimes it can be frustrating.

I was in the habit of operating from my own understanding and the knowledge that I managed to acquire from school and other resources. I was not leaning on the knowledge and wisdom of God until I fasted. It was not until I decided on July 30, 2017 to begin the 21 day no food fast and really surrender my ideas for how I wanted things to be, my goals for where I wanted to be financially, and how I wanted my relationships to be that I came to the place of peace and that easy yoke and light burden I had always desired, but never really let go enough to experience it. During these 21 days I had good days and not so good days. There were more good days than bad. This fast took me from the place of leaning on my own understanding and ability to do things to leaning on God's knowledge and wisdom and allowing Him to guide my hands, my mouth, my ministry, my business and everything else.

I say "my" loosely because it really all belongs to Him. He is just letting me hold it for the time that I am here. My whole life is His.

The sacrifice that Jesus made and the fact that He created me makes me and everything that I have or have access to His. My relationships are really His. My business, clothes, education, knowledge, gifts, talents, and my life are all His. I would have nothing, and I would be nothing if it were not for Him. It took some time for me to go from just knowing this. to believing it, which means to act on the knowledge that I have had for so long. I still wanted to control things. I still wanted to be the one to "figure things out." I still wanted to be the one to get things done according to my plan and according to the goals that I had set for my life. This was a major battle when it came to becoming a licensed minister. This was not in my plan or vision for my life. As far as I can remember it was not something that God told me would happen prior to around 2014-15 when people started to tell me I would become a minister or that I would preach.

As a Christian, I was always aware of the call to share and spread the Gospel. I did not have a problem with that. I never really had the desire to preach in front of the church. My calling I felt was to the world. So, the idea of becoming a licensed minister and preaching in the pulpit was the furthest thing from my mind, until He kept confirming it to me. I finally made the decision to be obedient and from there I ended up where I am today.

My life has been a tangled web that I have weaved, but I would not change any of it for the world. My story is my story and no one else's, my journey is my journey and no one else's, my life is my life and no one else's, and I am me and no one else. I am becoming comfortable and confident in just being who God called me to be so more life God-fident as I like to call it. I am God-fident that He does not make mistakes, that He does not make junk, and that I am created in His image. That in and of itself helps me to fight off those moments of insecurity and comparison that used to leave me down, envious, and depressed. I wanted that marriage my friend had, the cars my friends had, the children my friends had, and all of the things that were not

"It's All in Me!"

meant for me ever or at the time. I am learning to be like the Apostle Paul, content no matter what the situation. Other things that led to this transformation that I am experiencing today are working with my Life Coach and talking to her about my desires to build my business full-time and to have it be my primary source of income.

My Life Coach would encourage and hold me accountable. I was still inconsistent and had not really made up my mind that *Empowerment Unabridged* was going to be what I was going to do, no matter what. I knew what to do, but I just was not in the place where there was a sense of urgency for me to actually do it. I was more comfortable than I was content. I wanted to do things my way instead of God's way. I wanted things to look the way I wanted them to look and disregarded what God was trying to do and where God was trying to take me. I realized and started to internalize that partial obedience and disobedience due to not acting on something out of "fear" was still disobedience. There are consequences for disobedience. During this time, I was also still living a double life.

During my minister in training process I was going back and forth with sexual immorality and drinking alcohol to the point of drunkenness. I had not made a genuine decision to give those things up for good. As time progressed, I was able to be around people two days in a row who were drinking. Although I was tempted I did not give in to those temptations. I have decided that I will do what God has called me to do and be in His will no matter what other people are doing around me. I have made the decision to glorify God with my entire life and no longer make excuses for or justify my sin with the Word of God by saying that God knows my heart, I'm human, or that all sin and fall short of the glory of God. The fornication struggle has still been real. I have been disobedient and not sticking to boundaries trying to be supportive to my fiancée during his time of need. After the fire situation began to be taken care of I put the boundaries back in place again. Then my fiancée had a fraternity brother who was his college roommates commit suicide and a Pastor/mentor die four days apart from each other. So, the boundaries went away again, and fornication made a comeback. I am ashamed of how much I have taken God's grace for granted. God is working with us and has provided us with accountability, we have to use it.

In my life I was taught not to make excuses, so I didn't. My reasoning behind doing the things I was doing was simply because I wanted to. In using these reasonings I felt as if I was better than those that made those other excuses. It was my glorified way of sinning yet taking full responsibility for it. It did not make me any better, but to me I thought it did. Regardless of if I took responsibility for it or not, I was still sinning repeatedly every time I decided to masturbate, take a drink, have sex, curse someone out, lie, cheat, or anything else I was accustomed to doing, it was and is still sin. Truly taking responsibility for something means that you acknowledge it and make the necessary changes. I was not making the necessary changes. For me to break this cycle I had to fast and really make the sacrifice to kill my flesh and my messed-up beliefs about the things that I was doing. I read a 7-day devotional about fasting, although I was not fasting at the time, understanding more about it has helped me to understand the process God took me through during the 21-day fast. One devotional was as follows:

"It's All in Me!"

"When to Fast

When should we fast? Turn to Isaiah 58 and look at it verse-by-verse for the answers.

1. When caught in a sinful pattern. "Is this not the fast that I choose: to loose the bonds of wickedness . . ." When I can't seem to break out of a sinful pattern, I should fast (Isaiah 58:6).

2. When there is a heavy burden. "To undo the straps of the yoke, to let the oppressed go free, to break every yoke," (Isaiah 58:6).

3. When oppressed by the enemy. ". . . to let the oppressed go free," (Isaiah 58:6).

4. When we want to give to someone else. "Is the fast not to share your bread with the hungry and bring the homeless into your house?" (Isaiah 58:6).

5. When we need to be encouraged. "Then shall your light break forth like the dawn. Your healing shall spring forth

speedily and righteousness shall go before you. . ." (Isaiah 58:8).

6. When an answer to prayer is needed. "Then you should call, and the LORD will answer; you shall cry . . . and He will say: Here I am . . ." (Isaiah 58:9).

7. When we need to examine ourselves. "If you take away the yoke from your midst, the pointing finger and the spreading wickedness . . ." (Isaiah 58:10).

8. When we need direction. "And the LORD will guide you continually. . ." (Isaiah 58:11).

9. When we need spiritual restoration. ". . . And He will make your bones strong. You will be like a well-watered garden, like a spring of water whose waters do not fail," (Isaiah 58:11).

10. When we need revival. "And your ancient ruins will be rebuilt; you shall raise up the foundations of many generations . . ." (Isaiah 58:12).

"It's All in Me!"

Majority of these 10 things that were mentioned in this passage were signs that were occurring in my life telling me that I needed to fast. I would fast previously from social media, men, partial fasts, Daniel fast, and even a 5-day absolute fast, but never a 21-day absolute fast. There was an extended period that I needed to fast because there were a lot of things that God had to do in me during this time to prepare me for such a time as this. To prepare me to bear my soul to the world in this book. To prepare me to build *Jalisa Ray International* according to His will and plan and not my own. To prepare me to take the proper role and place in marriage and motherhood. Fasting is a phase of preparation. It may not be for you to do a 21-day fast but fasting is something that I can guarantee will change your life. Just a disclaimer it was a no food fast, not a 21-day water fast which I believe is very dangerous, but if God calls you to it then that is a different story. I was not called to that. I still took my *Youngevity's 90 For Life* nutritional supplements, drank lemon water, Kombucha, and towards the end, for many reasons, cranberry juice.

The healing crisis that I experienced during this time was not only physical, but spiritual and mental as well. I was literally fighting with myself throughout that time in all those aspects because my spirit, soul, and body wanted to stay comfortable instead of content with whatever the circumstances. Fasting took me out of my comfort zone and into the will of God for my life. The fast was not the only thing that I needed to do to deal with my issues of course, but it was a major part of the necessary transformation and transition in my life. I am still dying to my flesh. During the writing process of this book, I had a run in with my anger and I had to literally hold my hand over my mouth to keep from saying more than what I had already said. I know that growth occurred because prior to this fast I would have just let whatever was on my mind at the time fly out of my mouth. I would have no remorse until afterwards.

Minister Jalisa Ray

    This part of my journey, the 21-day fast, helped me to learn to do a lot of self-reflection and be more aware of myself and when God is speaking to me. I am more able to shut out distractions and focus on my tasks, praying, and people in conversations. I said in the midst of writing this book, "Maybe I need to fast again." This was because of my feelings towards my fiancée around that time. I allowed one small situation to turn into something bigger than it had to be and it caused us to not be on the best of terms. I realized that when it came to him that I fight in my flesh instead of in the spirit. When it came to him, I would curse first and pray later. I would get very angry and have to backup and evaluate why. This was so difficult for me to deal with because I made it a habit. I hung on to whatever the underlying beliefs were that caused me to act that way. I have worked with my counselor to get to the root of it because it was not healthy at all. I also realized that I would curse and yell at him because he allowed it. That I was the same way with God because He allowed me to sin I would take advantage of His grace. This was a tough pill to swallow but it is all a part of the renewal process.

    I love AJ. I know that I want to spend the rest of my life with him, so I had to deal with this to make the necessary changes in myself. I must take responsibility for it. Even if the things that bother me about him never change I am learning to respond in love. I must remember that no matter what I do I cannot change him. That even when I feel hurt that I am not the one to get vengeance for it. There is a part of me, my flesh, that still desires to get back at people, my fiancée, when I feel hurt. My way of doing so was showing anger and aggression, which was not helpful or healthy. This was how I managed to punch a hole in the wall. Instead of dealing with things appropriately I would let them build up and cause more damage than they should have. I am learning to pray quicker than I would have before, but again I am still a work in progress. I wish I could just snap my fingers and be fixed, but things aren't that easy. I know that if I did not have things that I needed God to

"IT'S ALL IN ME!"

continuously work on in me, that I would become arrogant and feel like I no longer needed God.

I will always need God no matter what. There will always be things for me to improve upon and things to learn. I know that I am not perfect. I do not want you to think that me sharing my journey is showing that I am perfect, and I have all the answers. I am not, and I do not. I often try to take things into my own hands. As far as AJ and I go, we are in therapy separately to deal with our individual challenges. I joined a few accountability groups. We are working on continuing premarital counseling. We had another person facilitating it, but she suggested that we go to my Pastor. He'll be the one marrying us, and his protocol is to see couples within 12 months of the wedding date. We are going back and forth with the idea of getting married in April or August of 2018. We'll see once we meet with my Pastor again. There is a lot going on with both of us and we still have arguments and disagreements. What keeps us together is our foundation in Christ and the confirmation we've received about each other. I have been doing better with my attitude and I have not cursed him out since my realization of why I do it.

We still have a lot of work to do. The strict boundaries I discussed earlier in the book come and go. The times they go, are the times we had sex. We are a work in progress but the goal for us to be married has not changed. We are working on following God's plan to get us there. We've started to do plans about marriage together on the *YouVersion* Bible App I mentioned. I completed the six stages of *The One University*. My therapist has given us marriage preparation assignments to do about finances and expectations. We argue much less, and the intensity of our arguments have decreased. I am more aware of what I say to be more gracious in my speech. I seek more to understand versus being understood so I ask questions for clarification. I am more aware of my emotions and evaluate them to see why I am feeling that way. My therapist gave me an assignment to speak affirmations to him at least once a day. This was something a friend of mine, Brittany Robinson, told me to do before but, I told you I'm hard headed. It worked wonders for both of us.

Previously in dealing with my negative emotions and feelings I would go back into my "fix it" mode trying to figure out how I could change it. I had to learn to stop myself, pray, and turn it over to God. No matter what I have done or tried to do my bad attitude towards and negative perception of my fiancée were only something God could fix. It helped to talk through it with my counselor. There were things God used her to show me.

God speaks in so many ways we just must be aware of them. A lot of times we miss His answers because He does not answer them in the manner or in the time frame we expect Him to. There was a process that required some discomfort and pruning to get to and remove the root of my attitude and negative emotions towards my fiancée. I will be the best wife and mother that I can be. I will not perpetuate the cycle of negative and non-submissive relationships that have been the predominant examples in my life. I want future generations and current generations to see a positive example of what a God-centered relationship looks like. Not what the media shows them or even other examples they may run across. I have great examples of marriages, but the bad examples of marriage are more memorable. That is something else I had to work on, seeing the positive aspects of relationships, instead of focusing on seeing the negative ones.

After all the blessings, promises manifested, trials, and tribulations I am still learning, growing, and maturing as I will be until the day I am called home. I am not where I want to be financially, but God has given me a gift and a plethora experience with helping people in order to do what God has called me to do with wealth coaching. Even when I get to where I want to be financially, there will be work that I must do to stay there and continue to grow financially. No, that does not make you, or me greedy, it's the natural progression of life to grow or to die. When you grow in other areas you grow financially. Money is just the store of value so the more value you create and bring to the world the more money you make. I will be in a place where I do give a lot, but I will also make sure to keep a lot as well to take care of my family and have things to pass down to future generations. I am building generational wealth.

I am on this same journey when it comes to my health, my relationships with God and others, and every other area of my life. There is always room to improve and grow. That is what I intend to do. I will not be the same person I am tomorrow that I am today. Every day I am growing, learning, changing, and maturing. I am grateful for who I was, and who I am today, because it has contributed to who I will be tomorrow. I will not always be snappy and rude and disrespectful when I feel hurt. I won't always have to use food stamps and state insurance. I won't always struggle with sexual immorality. I won't always feel inadequate about my knowledge pertaining to the Word and the things that God has called me to do. I won't always have daddy issues. I won't always eat and overeat when I am emotional, upset, or sad. I won't always feel the need to be validated by likes on social media. I won't always have a tough time hearing God's voice. I won't always get distracted while I am praying alone. I won't always eat unhealthy even when I know better. I won't always allow myself to make emotional and irrational decisions. I won't always be imperfect, but I won't be perfect until I make it to heaven. I always used to say that perfection is possible. I honestly do not want to be perfect here because as I said I know that if I ever get to the place where I have no struggles or issues that I will feel like I do not need God. Knowing what I do not know and knowing that there is always room for improvement, I am always striving to do better and always relying on God for it.

Where was I when it comes to *Jalisa Ray International* during the publishing process of this book?

Minister Jalisa Ray

This journey of building *Jalisa Ray International* has been amazing! I have learned, grown, and matured so much in a short amount of time. Being a full-time entrepreneur was one of the best decisions I had made for my life, of course being obedient to God's plan for my life. I love entrepreneurship, but I know that it may not be for everyone, at least to do it full-time. Everyone needs more than one stream of income, but a start-up business may not be for you. I have prepared for and done speaking, Spoken Word, and teaching engagements. I launched and relaunched a 5-Day Journey to Financial Freedom challenge, preparing to launch some new coaching programs, working with a web/graphic designer for my website and my line of merchandise, and have really allowed God to use me to bring the vision He has already completed to fruition in the present. I have been working with Kemberli Stephenson through *Mad Money University* to re-establish the foundation of *Jalisa Ray International*. I have been working with Genesis Dorsey through her *Coaching Queens* program to help me develop content for social media and additional products and programs. She brought me on as the leader of her finance and money mentorship program through *Led to Lead*. This was huge! I have not been trying to control things as much. I have not been worrying as much about what I look like on live videos. I have not been as self-conscious about my lisp. I have not been trying to fix the things that I feel are broken as much. Totally surrendering my life and the vision God has given me for *Jalisa Ray International* has been a journey within my life's journey. It is something that I have never done before but it feels like I should have been doing it all along. It brings me much more happiness and contentment with life. I have come to a place where I do not worry about my financial situation with this being the only source of income. God has been providing for me every step of the way. It has not come the way that I expected, but I have not had to worry or stress about things very long. I will get to a point soon where I do not worry or stress at all, but I haven't gotten there yet.

"It's All in Me!"

Since July 30, 2017, I have come a very long way! I enjoy the time freedom that I have. On the days where I do not feel like getting up or I know my body is telling me to rest I can without having to answer to someone else other than God. I decided to make Monday's my off days. On days where things come up with family and friends I can be there and adjust my schedule as needed. I am experiencing true freedom like I have never experienced before. Wealth is much more than just money. It is having freedom in every aspect of your life. *Jalisa Ray International* is helping me to see and achieve genuine wealth. It has really been tested and grown my faith. I am truly blessed to be in the position that I am in, to have the support village that I have on my journey of building *Jalisa Ray International*. Let me tell you about how my parents have been a tremendous blessing. When I was going through at my last job my mom was telling me to quit because I did not have to work at a job that I was miserable at. My parents do not mind their children being home, especially my mom. She wants us all to live together in a big house, spouses and children included. So, when I quit my job she told me not to worry about it. This was the same way the first job that I had quit when I became sick and depressed. My mom has always been supportive of my career decisions.

When it comes to *Jalisa Ray International* it has been no different. This journey even made me realize how much my dad pays attention to me. He knows when I am writing and when my speaking engagements are. He's asked me about the progress of my book and my business. There have been times when he was coming into my room and he said to my mom, "She's probably writing." He asks me about my events and engagements. I didn't realize how much he paid attention to me, but he does. This means the world to a girl with daddy issues. My mom has been super supportive with taking care of me. I take care of my supplements and my other business expenses, but I do not have to pay rent, phone bill, electricity, or water, until I build my business up to a livable wage. My parents have not pressured me to get another job even when they may struggle financially. My aunt who gave me my first car has even continued to pay my car insurance until I get things together. I would not be where I am if not for my family and friends. There have been so many people that have helped and supported me, and I am so very grateful.

Now that you know where I am, here's where I believe that God is taking me. So, as I continue to live out and share with the world you will see how things unfold. You'll see whether what I think or believe is going to happen. I am learning to walk in faith and not in sight, lean on God's understanding and not my own, and surrender to His path for my life instead of trying to make my own. Trying to create my own path has not worked for me at all. Trying to be a rebel and be different was not always beneficial for me. Even still, God always worked everything out for my good and His glory. I know that everything that is going to occur, for you and I, in our lives is already done.

I know that the work that He began in us is already completed. I know that when God created the Earth and everything in it He completed His work and declared that, "It is very good." I know that when Jesus died on the cross to overcome death, sin and the grave, He declared that that work He came to do on earth was finished. In knowing all of these things, I can imagine and expect that God will bless me exceedingly and abundantly above all that I could ask or think. I can walk in faith and believe that where I am now, there will only be an increase. I can walk in faith and know that the temporary things will be a blessing, but the eternal things they will not compare to. I have to constantly remind myself that these things are only temporary. In the moment they seem to be the worse or the best thing that could have happened to me.

Looking back, I know that a lot of things I made mountains, were molehills. Other things that I should have made into mountains from molehills, I did not. I know that my future will be greater than my present. It may be hard for me to see or believe right now, but I am standing on that belief, even if it waivers from time to time. My fiancée

"It's All in Me!"

and I had a rough time after the fire and things that were coming up in my life. We had a difficult time communicating. To me, it seemed like he had shut down on me and shut me out. I was on the verge of giving up and just quitting in that hard season. I wanted to retreat to my old ways of not caring and moving on with my life. Things were getting better. During our session with my pastor we established that we are together. That is why in this book I went from addressing him as my future husband to my fiancée. I was not sure what we were or what to call the place we were in, but we established that we are together.

Prior to us getting married, I felt, God wanted us to work on our individual things that we need to work on. To keep things in place so that we will not have sex prior to marriage, to help us work on things with our parents, and to get to a place with God where we are solely dependent on Him and not other things. My fiancée didn't like or agree with the idea of such strict boundaries, but I had to be obedient to what God was calling me to. The situation with the fire caused me to alter the initial agreement of us not seeing each other outside of sessions and to only talk once a month. Yes, those boundaries can be considered extreme. Most of the time we didn't stick to it anyway as far as us only talking once a month. It was what we needed for us to work on our individual challenges, to not have sex, and to work on our relationship with God. When it came to our relationship we had tried everything else to keep us from having sex and nothing else worked. So, it was necessary for us to take these extreme measures and set extreme boundaries for God to really do what He needed to do in and through us during our engagement. But, after the fire we started talking every day. It brought up some things that I was not expecting in both of us. It made it difficult for us to communicate and talk about the things that have been going on with us. I thought that things were getting better, and that God was going to help us get through this in a certain way. I thought that everything would be peaches and cream. The enemy had other plans. He was using us to get to each other and be distractions to one another causing a lot of friction between us. I cried a lot about things that happened between us. A lot of it had to do with us not being able to effectively express our feelings.

Instead of remaining positive and not taking things personally, I fed into the thoughts and the feelings that he did not care about me. That he was blowing me off. That he was doing things intentionally for us not to see each other or spend time together. I held onto negative thoughts and feelings to let them fester and get worse instead of addressing them to heal. I personally allowed the enemy to cause me to react negatively towards AJ. I know that this is exactly what the enemy wanted. In the moment I was driven by my emotions and I reacted instead of responded. I know that this is who God has for me, but in the midst of the mess. I missed the messages that God was trying to give me and almost gave up on the blessing that God has given me for the umpteenth time. Therefore understanding the future and plan that God has for me, not to harm me has been so important. I may not know everything, but I know that even in the midst of this situation with my fiancée and I, that it was not to harm me. I know that it will work out for our good and His glory. I was not able to see that before. I remembered it, but as soon as my emotions bubbled up and over, I allowed those negative thoughts and feelings to take me to places that I should not have.

I fed into those negative thoughts and words the enemy was speaking into my ear. I was acting out of selfishness and self-centeredness. I did not take as much time as I should have to see things from my fiancée's perspective and be more understanding of his situation. Although in the beginning I thought that he was going to be okay with the boundaries and the fire, I had unrealistic expectations of him. I expected that there wouldn't be times where he was not okay with it. I am so glad that I had my counselor during this time because in the midst of us arguing via text message, I went into a session and was able to talk through everything. I was able to understand what I have been doing wrong and how to move forward in a more effective way during

"It's All in Me!"

this season that we are in. Before my session I was analyzing things on my own, trying to figure out what to say and how to say it, fighting with myself between giving up and giving too much. Even praying and reading the Word, I was still on the verge of losing it. I was still on the verge of giving up on the future with my fiancée, that God has for us. She helped me to work through the things that occurred and see them from a different perspective.

I have to my flesh aside and fought this battle in the spirit. I am always reminded during these times that I tend to fight in my flesh when it comes to my fiancée. I thought that I had worked on that, but those situations I mentioned earlier showed me otherwise. Through those situations I was also able to see just how much I was still trying to fix things on my own before taking them to God. I end up messing things up more trying to fix them. Which is why this series of situations drained me so much. I was aware that I shouldn't, but being me, I just wanted things to happen now as opposed to later. I was being impatient with the process. If it were up to me, we would not have such strict boundaries. In my mind, I am like we know for sure that we are going to get married, but I knew the consequences and repercussions that could occur as well.

Our whole relationship was ruined the day that I decided that I would continue to pursue him sexually. I know that had we remained celibate all the drama and negativity that occurred between us would not have happened. I chose to go down that path of God's permissive will instead of accepting His perfect will for our relationship. I cannot do anything about that but take the route to His perfect will moving forward understanding that what I do daily impacts our future. I was not thinking about that at the time. I was more concerned with chasing the high I got from having sex and having all his attention on me. I understand that the future is now.

All I have is now, so for my future to come out better than my past and even my present, I have to make better decisions now. I know it is not the easy route, but my disobedience has made this route harder than it would have been if I was obedient. There were many times where I have had to make course corrections because I wanted to do things my way. I was willing to take on the consequences for the sake of what I wanted in the moment. It was the instant gratification that I wanted and still want really, that caused me to try to do things my way and not the way God intends for them to be done. I had become my own God, trying to take things into my own hands. I have jumped in and out of idolatry. I have jumped in and out of making myself my own idol feeling that I could take care of things better than God. As you can see from the events that occurred that this is still a journey for me. I know better for sure, but I lack the awareness in the moment, in the search of the instant gratification. I have been shifting my beliefs and my habits with this as well, so that I will not continue to go back to this pattern of idolizing myself. I do not know better than God. I cannot do better than God. I do not know myself better than God. I cannot fix myself or my situation better than God. I cause myself unnecessary headaches and heartaches trying to do so.

    Writing this book has brought me more awareness and will be a form of accountability once other people know my journey and my story. Going back over it to do edits was another reminder. Most of the time we know what to do, but reminders are necessary to keep us on track or to get us back on track. With the overload of information and opinions that we experience daily this is understandable. Certain things are deeper than that because we have a certain belief or system of beliefs that impact our actions. In this case it is deeper than that. The reminders are always helpful, but the true shift won't occur until I deal with the beliefs behind why I idolize myself. The beliefs behind why I feel that I can do a better job than God. The beliefs behind why I feel like I can take better care of myself than God. I know that my future is bright, but there will always be room for improvement, growth, and learning. I would not have it or want it any other way. Taking this journey called life with God having my life under control, and having already worked

"It's All in Me!"

everything out, makes life so much easier. When my life gets hard in the future I will know that I have taken on too much and have edged God out. *Did you catch that?* Edging God Out equals ego. I must get my ego out of the way and know that I am nothing, will be nothing, and will have nothing without Him. I know that I will not understand everything. I know that everything will not work out the way that I want them to, but I am learning to become okay with that. I am learning new things everyday even if I am unaware of the lessons.

I know I was a bit vague with some of the details of my future so let me give you a bit more detail. This again is what I believe that God will do in my future life. It will be interesting to come back to this in some years to see how much of this was really in God's will for my life. Some of these things I've mentioned before.

- This book will be a bestseller.
- The 5-Day Journey to Financial Freedom challenge will help thousands of people.
- I will continue to work on my health so that I will get rid of this acne and dry skin.
- I will pay off my student loan debt by 2020.
- I will get my business out of the red.
- I will be making livable wages from my business so that my business will eventually be a multi-billion-dollar company.
- In 2018, I will marry my best friend and we will probably conceive our first two children that night. Yes, twins. A boy and a girl, God willing.
- I will continue to travel and do speaking engagements and workshops.
- Eventually, I will be traveling all over the world speaking, preaching, teaching, and coaching.
- I will be the author of 20 or more books.

- AJ and I will continue to have children and do ministry together, whether it be with the business, couples ministry, dealing with children or anything else.
- I will have the freedom to be at home with my children and even homeschool them if we'd like.
- We will be able to take family trips and go do things freely.
- I will be able to retire my parents by 2020.
- I will be able to see both of my little brother's Dante and Demetrius go off to college, then the NFL, and go to their games all over the world.
- My family and I will be able to have a big house or a cull de sac of houses that we own for us to live in.
- My family and I will be and stay debt free. Not just these generations but future generations.
- My family will not have to continue to deal with and suffer from major ailments and diseases. We will live long healthy lives.
- We will farm and raise our own food and meat. I will have holistic healthcare practices all over the world.

Some of these things will happen, some may not, but my expectation and belief are for them to occur and more. I know that I have a bright future ahead of me even in the midst of dark days. I reached my 55,000-word goal for this book. Did it seem like that many words? Did it seem like more? In the beginning of this journey when I asked my business coach how long a book normally is, and she said 55,000 I almost passed out. Once I set the date, picked the time to write every day and made it a habit these 55,000 words took no time at all. This principle applies to everything in my life. I have been able to break down other tasks and get them done daily using this same concept. In the midst of writing my book, I was able to get so many other things done. This all goes back to my faith, where I surrendered to God's will for my life. This for me has been the easier path. I did not say it is easy, but it is

"It's All in Me!"

easier than trying to do things on my own. I know that God has been and will be with me along the way.

There were days I was tired and drained because of other things going on in my life, but I kept pushing forward. The enemy wanted me to stop, to not get this out to you, to not work on the challenge for you. To eat unhealthy because of how I was feeling. To just lay down and not do anything, but the devil is a liar and already defeated! I have finished writing and publishing this book. I have launched and relaunched the challenge. I continue to feed my mind with positivity. I am successful. I am victorious, and I am an overcomer! It is funny how I can be encouraging and pouring into one of my clients but sometimes have a tough time encouraging myself. You may be in a place where you want to give up. You may be in a place where your feelings are holding you hostage or in bondage. You may be in a place where you do not know what to do but this book and my story has hopefully been an inspiration and a motivation to you. You have the faith, friends/family, the ability to forgive/forget, things to feed your mind with, and the Guide to show you what path to take. It may mean getting out there and changing your circle. It may mean getting a different book or finding someone new to follow. It may mean getting a therapist, life coach, business, coach or accountability partner. It may mean forgiving that person that you felt was unforgivable and forgetting what they did to you or forgetting the effect that it had on you. It may mean going back and evaluating where your faith really lies. Is your faith in the enemy prevailing in your life bigger than the faith that you have in the plan that God has for your life? It may mean removing some people from your life and from your circle. It may mean setting boundaries and watching people leave on their own. It may mean getting rid of the things that are feeding your flesh instead of your spirit like television shows, social media, and the like. It may be all of the above.

The thing about it is if you do not allow God to lead you on your pursuit to freedom and living abundantly everything that you do will be in vain. You will do the work, but without the faith in God it is in vain. I was given an illustration one day in our Young Adult Ministry Bible study and it has stuck with me, so I want to share it with you. The teacher gave the illustration of God having us follow Him in a room with our eyes closed. In the room there may be a table, chairs, and anything else. Instead of us keeping our eyes closed we peek to make sure that we do not run into anything. If we see something that we may run into we stop or try to change directions on our own. Instead of seeing what God would do and trusting with blind faith that He has our best interest in mind and will make sure we get what we need to get out of being in that room. He may split the table in half for us to walk through it, move us in another direction at the last minute, or He may even let us run into it. But all of it He will work out for our good and His glory. We never know exactly how God is going to work things out and we do not always understand why things happen but that's what faith is for to trust Him in spite of the uncertainties. To trust Him in spite of the pain and/or discomfort you may feel. You have everything that you need to succeed in life and holiness. Once you are saved you have the exact same Spirit within you that raised Jesus from the dead.

> You can overcome anything!

> Nothing is stronger than that power!

> Nothing in your life will stand a chance against it!

Tapping into that power means surrendering to it. Making it so that sin is not an option. It means essentially becoming a true slave to Christ where the only option that you will even entertain in your life is the direction that God gives you. There are so many more things that God will be able to do with you once you move out of your own way. Again, I am still learning this, so I am giving you what God has given me for the both of us. He wants every part of us and to have control over every part of our lives. He wants that because He wants nothing but the best for His children. The thing is He will not force you to allow Him to

"It's All in Me!"

be in control. He wants us to give Him control. To let go of the controls and step aside for Him to do what He does. For Him to complete the work He began and completed an eternity ago. We still have an eternity to go. *Is your life and eternity going to be in freedom and living abundantly or in bondage, sin, and living a mediocre existence?* You have a choice and you have what it takes to do either or. *What are you going to do with it? Are you going to live in hell and then die and go to hell? Or are you going to bring Heaven to Earth until Heaven is on Earth?* I have shared with you my story from start to finish. Where I am now, where I was, and where I am headed.

I hope that my story has blessed you just as much as writing it and sharing it with you has blessed me. I do not mind being naked and exposed for the glory of God and for other's souls. This is part of my purpose, calling and ministry. Your story is part of yours. *How will you use it? Are you still ashamed to share it?* It's not about you. It is about the people that God has assigned you to, to help lead them to Him You have a calling and a purpose that only you can fulfill. You can share my story and share your story, but I want to make sure that you are free and living abundantly. So, make sure to connect with me on Facebook, like my Facebook Page (*Minster Jalisa Ray*), subscribe to my YouTube page, and subscribe to my mailing list so you can continue to hear my story and how it unfolds. I hope and pray that my story and my journey blessed you and continues to bless you. I look forward to hearing and/or seeing your story unfold for the glory of the Lord. I will end by sharing a letter I wrote for you. You may have already heard or read this somewhere but this is my heart's desire for your life and why I want to continue to walk with you on your journey to freedom and living abundantly.

Minister Jalisa Ray

Dear Queen or King that I may or may not know,

You have a purpose that only you can fulfill. You do not have to keep settling for less the way I did for so long. You do not have to hide or run from your past, that doesn't define you. The things that people took from you will be restored. It is time for you to experience the easy yoke and light burden that God has for you. If only you would surrender and let go of the things you thought had you bound. You are free because, "Whom the Son sets free is free indeed." There is no question about your freedom. Freedom, wealth, and holistic health are a part of your destiny. It was not by happenstance that you came across this. Jesus said He's come that you, YES YOU, might have life and have it more abundantly! Are you ready to walk into your more abundant life? Take my hand, let's go! We can take this journey together, you do not have to do it alone! With God, you, and I, you cannot, will not, shall not fail! The tactics of the enemy will not prevail! You're victorious and he's defeated! It's time for you to win! Your time is NOW to walk the true path on your journey to freedom and living abundantly!

www.ingramcontent.com/pod-product-compliance
Lightning Source LLC
Chambersburg PA
CBHW071925290426
44110CB00013B/1473